THE ESSENTIAL
A-Z
OF
CREATIVE WRITING

THE ESSENTIAL

A-Z

OF
CREATIVE WRITING

Nancy Smith

CASSELL

For Jan Rae who suggested I write this book. For Crediton Writers' Circle which sprang from my first writing class and for all my students, past and present, who have in their turn taught me so much.

Cassell Publishers Limited
Artillery House, Artillery Row,
London SW1P 1RT

First published 1989

British Library Cataloguing in Publication Data

Smith, Nancy
  The essential A-Z of creative writing
  1. Creative writing – Manuals
  I. Title
  808′.042

  ISBN 0-304-31804-3

Typeset by St George Typesetting, Pool, Redruth, Cornwall
Printed and bound in Great Britain by Biddles Ltd,
Guildford and King's Lynn

Contents

'The Word creates everything, all that we love and hate, the totality of being. Nothing exists before it has been uttered in a clear voice.'

(Inscribed in hieroglyphs on stone beside the Nile nearly five thousand years ago.)

Acknowledgements

The author wishes to thank all those writers whose words, quoted in this book, add so much by way of example and illustration: in particular, the extracts from the following: *The Man Who Loved Squirrels*, H.E. Bates, from the collection *The Song of the Wren*, reprinted by permission of William Heinemann Ltd.; *Afternoon of a Good Woman*, Nina Bawden, published by Macmillan Ltd., and reprinted by permission of Curtis Brown Ltd.; *The Woman Destroyed*, Simone de Beauvoir, by permission of Collins Publishers; *Katie Mulholland*, Catherine Cookson, by permission of Macdonald & Co. (Publishers) Ltd.; *Nile*, Laurie Devine, by permission of André Deutsch Ltd.; *A Child in the Forest*, Winifred Foley, by permission of BBC Enterprises Ltd.; *The Day of the Jackal*, Frederick Forsyth, by permission of Century Hutchinson Ltd.; *In Search of a Character*, Graham Greene, by permission of The Bodley Head Ltd.; *The Realities of Fiction*, Nancy Hale, by permission of Macmillan Ltd.; *Writers at Work: The Parish Review Interviews*, Ernest Hemingway and Georges Simenon, by permission of Martin Secker & Warburg Ltd.; *The Lion*, Joseph Kessell, by permission of Editions Gallimard; *Danse Macabre*, Stephen King, by permission of Macdonald & Co (Publishers) Ltd.; *The Road to Lichfield* and *A Stitch in Time*, Penelope Lively, both by permission of William Heinemann Ltd.; *The Art of Writing*, André Maurois, by permission of Curtis Brown Ltd.; *Story Writing*, Edith Ronald Mirrielees, by permission of The Writer Inc.; *Politics and the English Language*, George Orwell, by permission of Martin Secker & Warburg Ltd.; *Daily and Sunday*, Richard Powell, by permission of Curtis Brown, New York; *The East of Eden Letters*: *Journal of a Novel*, John Steinbeck, by permission of William Heinemann Ltd.; *The Moonspinners*, Mary Stewart, by permission of Hodder and Stoughton Ltd.; *Daydreams and Nightmares*, Dylan Thomas, by permission of J.M. Dent & Sons Ltd.

Special thanks are also due to Sue Townsend, and the authors who kindly provided the 'Top Tips' for this book – Catherine Cookson, Sara Craven, Margaret Thomson Davies, Tessa Krailing, Rhona Martin and Janet Rae.

Foreword

We've all seen those advertisements in the sort of Sunday news-papers we deny reading: 'Make £s writing for TV and films! You too can be a writer! Send only a thousand pounds for our *Creative Writing Course* and in six short months you could be jostling elbows with Kingsley Amis at grand literary lunches. Yes! Fame, riches and publishers' advances could all be yours!'

Years ago these advertisements used to be illustrated by a photograph of a smug-looking man with a short back and sides haircut. He was clenching a pipe between his strong white teeth. He looked to me as though he had never had an original idea in his life.

Nancy Smith's book brings the subject of writing for publica-tion down to where it belongs – earth. It is a sensible, practical book which should inspire timid would-be writers to get crack-ing and actually *start*. Starting is the hardest part. I should know; it took me twenty years before I dared to show my stuff. I now own the largest collection of unpublished writing in Eng-land. Cardboard box after cardboard box full of it is stored in my cellar.

The Essential A-Z of Creative Writing is full of good advice and is written in a clear, friendly style which neither intimi-dates the beginner nor patronises the more experienced writer. I wish the book well and hope that its readers will be encour-aged enough to offer their work and have the great pleasure of seeing it published or performed.

It is hard-nosed world out there, but faint-hearted writers should remember that there is an insatiable demand for *original* talent. Don't wait twenty years as I did, life is far too short.

Sue Townsend *Leicester*

Introduction

True ease in writing comes from art, not chance. As those move easiest who have learn'd to dance.

Alexander Pope

One of the most wonderful aspects of taking up writing as a hobby (as opposed to thinking of it in terms of a career, at this stage) is that you can begin at my age. You need only three things: a love of words, some means of setting them down (pen and paper, a typewriter or even a tape-recorder will suffice) and imagination. Lack of a formal higher education is no barrier.

Many of you will be taking those first stumbling steps on the writing road, with no map to guide you. You may be well on into your 40s or 50s. If you are a woman, possibly your family has grown up and left home, leaving you free to pursue your dream of becoming a writer. If a man, you may have recently retired and wish to fulfil that same dream, which you have had for many years. Perhaps you have led an exceptionally interesting life and wish to tell others about it. Whatever your reason for wanting to express yourself in words, you will probably have been good at English at school (particularly 'composition' as it used to be called), or you send long descriptive letters to friends who comment on how much they enjoy receiving them. You may have scribbled in secret for years, too shy to show your work to anyone, or you may have been submitting it to editors or publishers for a very long time, receiving mostly rejections and not understanding why.

There are two questions that all teachers of creative writing are asked, at some time or other: Can writing be

1

taught? Does one have to write for money rather than just for pleasure?

In answer to the first, whilst talent is something you are born with (and no amount of teaching can provide that), if you do have it, there is no question but that you can be helped to hone it and to acquire skills more quickly than you would by struggling on your own. If you take up pottery, painting, woodwork, cookery or sewing, you expect to learn certain techniques in order to become proficient, so why should not the same be true of writing? Writing is a craft as well as an art. I once asked a successful painter whether he liked to be known as a painter or an artist. His reply was that he referred to himself as a painter and hoped someone else would call him an artist. I think this view is also appropriate to writers.

As to whether or not one should aim at publication, i.e. do it for money, I believe that, if what you have written is good, be it long or short, you will want an audience. Exactly *which* audience needs to be considered carefully and will be discussed at various points in this book.

By all means, write for your own enjoyment because the act of creating, of bringing into being of something that did not exist before, gives us humans our most intense and primary satisfaction. But, granted that we can gain much pleasure purely from the act of writing creatively, if we are sincere about wishing to do so to the best of our ability, then we will probably not be content with merely pouring out words onto paper. We will want an audience. To gain one entails polishing and re-arranging our words until, at last, our writing sparkles with colour and life and is a delight to read as well as being a clear communication of our meaning. When we have attained this standard of near-perfection (we never feel we've achieved it completely), then we are on the way to being able to call ourselves 'a writer'.

On the subject of needing an audience André Maurois has written:

Why is it so necessary for a writer to have a public? If his purpose is to express himself, ought it not to be enough for him that he should succeed in doing so? Is a cloud of witnesses really essential? He, the writer, has written with the deliberate purpose of revealing the truth about himself and about the world as he sees it. The revelation can have no point unless it reaches those for whom it is intended.

The Art of Writing (Bodley Head)

I hope that when you have reached the end of this book you will feel you have, at the least, a useful map to help you find your way to success.

Action

Raymond Chandler once gave this advice: 'If the story flags, bring in a man with a gun.' This was his way of saying that to hold a reader's attention a story needs to have plenty of action. Something must *happen* and go on happening to make the reader keep turning those pages. However beautifully descriptive the setting, however interesting the characters, unless some action is taken by someone, the story will flag and the reader will put the book down and pick up another.

Long passages of philosophising, of detailed descriptions of background are just what most of us skip in books that were either written a century ago or are by well-known names who 'get away with it'. Action, and as soon as possible, is vital if the reader's attention is to be held, and is one way of 'hooking' him instantly, of dragging him into the story almost unawares. Our word 'drama' is from the Greek root meaning 'to do'. Keeping this point in mind should help ensure that our characters are actively engaged in doing something rather than merely talking or thinking for a large part of our story.

My daughter was quite young and already an avid reader at around the time when Enid Blyton was first being frowned upon by librarians and educationalists. I well remember her reaction when I told her of their attitude. 'But, Mum,' she protested, 'something's always *happening* in her books!' Surely wisdom from the mouth of a babe, and worthy every would-be fiction writer remembering.

The article

This is a short piece of prose, basically factual in content though perhaps slightly embroidered and sometimes employing fictional techniques to make it more readable.

Most writers begin by trying their hand at articles of the kind where the personal viewpoint predominates as opposed to 'straight' feature articles. These might be nostalgia, personal experience, self-help based on personal knowledge (e.g. 'How I overcame agoraphobia') humorous or 'how-to' pieces. Another useful starting point is the 'anniversary' article. Magazines are always looking for these on, for example, St Valentine's Day, Hallowe'en, Christmas and, more especially, lesser-known interesting anniversaries. What editors want is well-researched information written up in an entertaining way. What they do *not* want is the same-old-mixture-as-before served up yet again. They seek originality: new content or a fresh angle.

Starting off your writing life with articles rather than short stories makes sense for several good reasons. Their structure is much simpler so they are easier to write; there is a ready market for good material from the freelance; and an acceptance – far more likely in the case of an article than a short story – will boost your morale and encourage you to continue.

Contrary to popular belief, it does not follow that, being gifted with a fertile imagination, you will be able to toss off short stories with little or no effort. The chances are that, if you begin with these (and some of you may have discovered this already) you will become discouraged by rejection after rejection with the result that your confidence will be severely shaken, possibly gone forever. Even after selling your first piece you've a long way to go before you can properly regard yourself as a writer, but at least you will have proved to yourself that you can put down words on paper for which someone is willing to pay good money.

A woman student of mine, 'just' a housewife for forty years, joined an Adult Education creative writing class to keep her grey matter active and because she had long nourished a secret desire to write. She had also taken up sailing because it was her husband's retirement hobby and was persuaded to write a piece on their experiences canal-cruising in France – which she quickly sold to a monthly boating magazine. Her self-confidence, she was the first to admit, grew out of all proportion to the size of the cheque she received, and she then embarked on a humorous autobiographical novel on sailing.

Here are some points to remember on writing articles.

1   Writing must have form, and the sooner you realise this the quicker you are likely to achieve success. Structure is a word that should be engraved on your brain. Visualising an article as having a diamond shape may help you impose form. The beginning should tell the reader exactly what it is about: make its theme apparent. The middle is where you should expand the facts and enliven the article with anecdotes, quotes and vivid descriptions. The end should return to the beginning to 'round it off'. An illustration of this 'diamond shape' is shown at the end of this section.

2   The maxim 'One theme, one article' is a good one to keep in mind. For example, if you are writing about paper, its uses and how it is made, stick to that: don't sidetrack about trees and other products made from them.

3   Information must be up-to-date. You will have to do some research to ensure this.

4   Always try to present information in a striking way. For example give meaning to any statistics by helping your reader picture them: 'X number of trees were felled in Britain in 1988 which, if laid down end to end, would go X number of times round Britain.'

5   Try to find a 'peg' on which to hang your article, linking it to something topical. When the *Mary Rose* was brought to the surface, a few years ago, a sailor's shoe was found inside, virtually intact. A man with a life-time's knowledge of the cobbling trade wrote an article on shoes and sold it to a Hampshire magazine, cleverly using the discovery of the *Mary Rose* as his 'peg'. No doubt he could also have used the same material, given it another angle and emphasis and found a quite different outlet, a shoe-trade magazine possibly.

My own first acceptance (one never forgets that one) resulted from some research I had done into the myths and legends connected with Santa Claus. The writers' circle to which I belonged had set this theme for 'homework'. I was very much a beginner and knew nothing about 'pegs' but my piece was bought by a newspaper (for 12/6d) and, after slight sub-editing, appeared on December 5th – the Eve of St Nicholas – thus giving it topical appeal.

6   Remember the need to entertain the general reader (that is if you are not writing a specialist/technical article), who does not want an unrelieved diet of facts.

7   Be specific, bearing in mind another useful maxim: 'If you don't know, find out. If you can't find out, leave it out.' Never use words or phrases suggesting uncertainty, such as 'possibly', 'it might', 'I think', etc. unless you qualify with something like: 'To this date, no one has found any evidence', or 'and so it is open to conjecture'. This makes it plain that it isn't just yourself who doesn't know, no one else does either.

8   A good lead-sentence or 'hook' is vital to inform a reader what the article is about and persuade him to continue. Opening with a question can be very effective. See example on page 11. You must then end either with a statement (as in the example) or with another question, which in this case could be: 'So, having considered the pros and cons, what is your answer? Will *you* be buying any toy guns for presents this Christmas?'

9   Strong feelings about something can offer a good basis for an article, provided you don't simply express your own opinions. The only time you can expect to sell these is when they are requested for particular slots, such as *The Lady*'s 'Viewpoint' or *Choice*'s occasional 'Opinion' page. Otherwise, you must back them up with facts, figures and the authoritative words of experts.

10   An eye-catching title is important: one which encapsulates your subject matter. Alliterative titles have considerable impact. 'Sun, Sea and Sand in Sinai' was one such sold by a student of mine. Clearly, it was about holidaying in Sinai. Puns are also useful. 'Cooking Granny's Goose' in a Christmas number promises to be a humorous piece about roast goose for dinner which, quite probably, doesn't turn out as intended. If you can't immediately hit upon a title with eye-appeal, don't be tempted to use something uninspiring, like 'A Holiday In Sinai' or 'Christmas With Granny'. The editor might take one look at it and chuck it on the reject pile, without reading any further. A dull title shrieks 'amateur'. If you are serious about learning your craft, you must aim for professionalism.

11   'Milk' your own knowledge for all its worth, in fiction as well as non-fiction. One young student of mine kept horses and also taught teenagers with personality problems. Within a year of taking up writing she was selling non-fiction pieces to equestrian magazines and short stories to magazines catering for teenage girls.

If you have a hobby in which you consider yourself something of an expert, it is likely that you can produce saleable articles of the 'how-to' kind, always remembering you are aiming to teach someone how to improve their efficiency in that particular field.

12   It is important to get your length right. A good average length, suitable for many markets, is 600-800 words but, as always, you should study the publication at which you are aiming. If it carries only 1500-word articles, then that is what

you must give, so long as you have sufficient material to sustain that length. Otherwise find another outlet. However, by doing some research (likely to be necessary in most cases), you may find you have enough information to expand (*not* pad) to the required length.

13   Once you have decided upon your subject and slant, then brainstorm, i.e. list quickly in very brief 'headings' anything and everything that has any bearing on your topic. When you have finished, the next step is to assemble all or some of the points into a suitable order. Here you might even find it helpful to write each one on a separate piece of paper and juggle them round like a pack of cards until they form an effective sequence. When this has been achieved and you've come up with your lead-sentence (and perhaps a good title) you are ready to begin creating.

14   Avoid liberal use of the personal pronoun. It irritates a reader to be constantly reading 'I'. Also avoid repetition of words wherever possible (a thesaurus will help here) as this too becomes irritating.

15   On the question of when to submit your article(s), be aware of publishers' requirements. Weekly magazines need 'copy' submitted six weeks before the date of issue; monthlies at least three months and, in the case of Christmas numbers, six months before. An anniversary article aimed at a daily newspaper should be sent in six to eight weeks beforehand to give the editor time to consider if he might find a slot for it.

Finally, here is an exercise that should help you produce that first saleable article:

Study newspaper and magazine articles about anniversaries, such as St Valentine's Day, Easter, May Day, Midsummer, Hallowe'en, Guy Fawkes Night, Christmas and New Year, to name only the most obvious. Also look out for articles on birth or death anniversaries of famous figures. This will give you an idea of the sort of thing being published and will suggest possible markets for your own work. Next, thinking at least six months ahead, go to your library and spend several hours researching your chosen topic, at the same time looking for a different or unusual angle.

Write your first draft, then begin pruning, polishing and re-writing as often as is required to produce that original, fresh piece that will be snapped up by the first editor to whom you send it. The earlier you start researching, writing up and sending out your article, the better your chance of success, because others will be doing likewise.

And, yes, I *did* say articles are easier than fiction!

To buy, or not to buy, toys of violence, this Christmas?

Is it
morally
right to give
a child a toy gun
for Christmas present?

Anecdote about how own small
son made a tommy-gun for himself
from a branch of a tree. Quote
from psychologists and others as well as
other anecdotes to add interest

My son will definitely
not be finding a
toy gun in his
stocking this
Christmas.

Top Tip from Janet Rae

Author of *Quilts of the British Isles and Ireland,* (Constable, 1987) and joint author of *Guide to Traditional Crafts of Scotland* (Chambers, 1988).

Feature writing for newspapers and magazines can be a good starting point for would-be writers. The chances of being published are greater than in fiction and the discipline of writing a good piece, in a way that is both economical and interesting, is excellent practice for other forms of composition.

Good features have a distinct structure, the two most important characteristics being a strong, short opening paragraph and a well-rounded ending. A lively and informative style is also vital to hold the reader's interest.

Ideas for features are all round you. You needn't think an interview with Sir Alec Guinness or the Prime Minister essential to a successful sale. A novice who wishes to develop feature-writing skills must learn his craft by first looking for stories 'close to hand'. If growing rhododendrons from seed is your hobby, then try writing about it; if you have developed an original knitwear design or tied a fantastic trout-fly, then write about that.

Do-it-yourself articles or interviews with unusual craftsmen/women in your own locality could easily provide you with a saleable article for your local newspaper or a specialist magazine. Similarly, if your interest is Chinese cooking or bonsai, healthy-eating or dovecots, try your hand at finding an unusual angle to your subject and write about it.

Autobiographical writing

There is a saying that God created people because He loves stories. There is another that everyone has at least one book in them. The latter is certainly true because each of us has at least our own story to tell, which will be of interest to someone, if only our immediate family.

Currently, there is a growing interest in this form of writing. Perhaps it springs from a desire to search for one's roots, to see the pattern of one's life emerge from the dense undergrowth of life's vicissitudes, understand it and thus gain new insight and a deepening sense of identity. For this reason alone, to write one's own story has value, leaving aside all thought of possible publication.

We have lived through such dramatically-changing times that, if we put our memories onto paper, we end up with what is virtually a document of social history. If, at the time of our birth, any seer had forecast that the 1970s would see a man walking on the moon, he would have met with laughter and if, in fifty years' time, our descendants should pick up and read our book, they will doubtless find it hard to believe some of the things about our way of life.

Having accepted, therefore, that writing your own personal history has value both to yourself and your family, what about the general public? The honest answer is that it will not be of wide appeal unless you have led an exceptionally unusual life and/or have achieved notoriety or distinction in some particular field. However, if you can write about an ordinary sort of existence with humour and feeling, making it so vivid that we see a particular region or strata of society as if it were floodlit, then you might well reach a wider audience. There are many instances of this: Margaret Powell's *Below Stairs* and Winifred Foley's *A Child in the Forest*, for example. The Dirk Bogardes and Peter Ustinovs will always command a readership and find a publisher. If you've done something as outlandish as Lucy Irvine in answering an newspaper advertisement and marrying a total stranger in order to spend a year on a deserted island, provided you have a reasonably good style and can write graphic descriptions of both the island and the difficulties you encountered, as she did in *Castaway*, then you will also probably find someone willing to publish it. James Herriot's vet books and Derek Tangye's about escaping from the rat race to grow flowers in Cornwall all caught the public's imagination. Reading and studying such books will help you see how to tackle your own to make it entertaining as well as honest.

Even fiction is to some extent autobiographical, in that we draw upon our emotions and experiences, our thoughts and desires, which provide a rich vein of material if we are brave enough to use it, and help us to find our own writing voice. Catherine Cookson, one of Britain's best-selling authors, has achieved phenomenal success by drawing upon her childhood memories of Tyneside, seventy years ago, and fictionalising them. Her most moving book, however, *Our Kate*, is a true account of her illegitimacy and growing up with the woman, an alcoholic, whom she thought to be her sister but who was, in fact, her mother – Kate; a woman she couldn't bring herself to call 'Mam' until late in life. (Incidentally, this book took twelve years to write and went through eight drafts.) But, in digging up our past in an attempt to put down on paper everything about our life, warts and all, a good deal of buried pain may well emerge, which will be all the better for being brought to the surface. The recovery of memories is often a healing process and is a basic technique of psychotherapy.

But, at this stage, you are merely consumed by the urge to write about your life for your own satisfaction: so where to begin? Must it be with your birth, about which you obviously know nothing except what you have learned from parents or older siblings? Must it be told chronologically? The answer to both questions is: not necessarily. In order to get yourself started it's probably best to find a period that has special significance for you and begin there. One such might be an episode which you later realised was an important turning point in your life.

As memories begin to emerge, small, long-buried incidents and seemingly trivial details will come to the surface. Don't discard these as being of no account because it is just such trifles that will add colour and substance to your story.

One student, a lady of seventy, writing about her early childhood in India where her father was a sergeant in the Indian Army, referred in passing to a *punkah*, not realising that not everyone knew what this was and that it would interest us to have one described so we could *see* it. Gradually, week after week, as this lady became immersed in her story, her work became more alive as she fleshed out with small details various touching, amusing or frightening incidents involving servants and ponies, illnesses and schooling, food, plant and animal life on the North West frontier. Sensing the interest of her audience during one manuscript reading, she went on to relate an incident that was, she said, as clear to her then, nearly sixty years later, as if it were in a snapshot in front of her. On a picnic, she told us, a vulture had swept down and snatched a sandwich from her hand. 'Put that in your book,' everyone cried.

It is important to be specific in order to make your story evocative. Never use an abstract word such as 'beautiful' to describe the day, for instance. Even if you can't remember exactly what it was like, you'll have an image in your mind's eye of the sun shining in a cloudless blue sky – so describe it like that. It will re-create your mood at the time, even if not the accurate state of the weather. This extract from Penelope Lively's *A Stitch in Time* (Puffin Books, 1986) shows how mood and weather can be firmly established in only a few words:

Not, Maria thought, a straightforward lovely day with a boring blue sky and nothing in it but the sun, but better than that because the sky was pleasantly busy with clouds, huge shining heaps of cloud that roamed across the horizon, ebbed and flowed, formed and reformed as you watched them. And every now and then they blotted out the sun for a few minutes: so that bands of sunshine fled along the coastline...everything would go grey and muted as the sun went in, and there would be this band of golden colour sweeping along the cliffs to Weymouth, lighting up now a bright slice of rock, now a green field, now the white sparkle of a house, now the turquoise of the sea itself.

Important aids to recall are photographs and family documents, which can also be reproduced to enhance your text.

In almost every writing class I have run at least one member has already begun, or has wished to begin, work on their autobiography and, always, the rest of the group has followed its progress with growing absorption. One related her growing up in comparative poverty in a Welsh mining village with a father, a conscientious objector in the First World War, who went on to become a well-known protagonist for miners' rights. There was the Indian childhood I have mentioned. Another member wrote on living in India at the time of Partition and the end of the British Raj, while another described a Victorian-style girlhood and life in a boarding-school that sounded more like something out of Dickens than Angela Brazil. One student was tracing her family tree and writing up what was, in essence, a social history of several generations of Yorkshire men and women. In the process, these students also developed their writing skills, improved their style and gave endless hours of pleasure both to themselves and to those of us privileged to listen to their manuscripts being read aloud.

Having finished your first draft, then comes the re-writing and that most important part of all, getting a good opening that will hook your reader. Let's take a look at how Winifred Foley began *A Child In The Forest*.

At home, I was 'our Poll' to my little sister and brother; 'my little wench' to Dad; 'a regular little' oman' sometimes but often a 'slumucky little hussy' to my sorely tried Mam; to the ribald boys, 'Polish it behind the door' and to my best friend Gladys – just 'Poll'. Gladys was an only child, always clean and tidy, but she never turned up her nose at playing with me, even when the school nurse found lice in my hair and my neck was covered with flea bites.

I was born in 1914, the fourth child of....

Who could resist carrying on reading a book that begins like that?

To move from beginnings to endings, what do we do with our treasured manuscript when it is finally completed to the best of our ability? I believe this is one of the few instances when so-called 'vanity-publishing' (q.v.) is justified, though it need not be in an expensive way. Depending upon the length of your script and the number of copies required, you should be able to find a printer in your locality who would, for the sum of somewhere between £250 and £500, produce it in the form of a booklet which you can then distribute amongst family and friends. However, do spend time choosing a suitable typeface, and ask to see a sample printed page before committing yourself. You don't want to be disappointed with the result. You may find that with the outlay of a few more pounds you can improve the quality of the end-product which, with today's ever-improving technology, can be quite professional. One enterprising seventy-year-old I knew produced her own autobiography in this way and then asked a number of shops to put it on sale in return for a small commission. Eventually she recouped the entire cost as people living in the neighbourhood as well as visiting holiday-makers bought it for its local interest.

It may take you months or years to do justice to the way you see your lifetime and you may have to accept that no one, beyond your family and friends, will want to read it, but you will have written an honest, lively account of many years spanning part of a century that has seen incredible changes. You will be able to say: this is me – I have existed.

A good memory is the key to autobiographical writing. The ten points that follow will help you trigger off memories that, if you think around them long enough, will provide lots of material for you to work on.

1   Think back to when you were a child and try to recall an important incident or event. Imagine you are six or seven: was there a traumatic experience that now begins to resurface? Try to get to know that child once again.

2   School. Do you remember your first day at infant, junior, high school or boarding-school? Was there one teacher whom you loved, hated or feared?

3   Illnesses. Can you remember what they were, if you were treated by the doctor or your mother or hospitalised, perhaps?

4   Games. What games did you play after school? They seemed to go in fashions, I recall – hoops, skipping-ropes, yo-yos, marbles and so on.

5   Holidays and travel.

6   The War. How did it affect you? Were you evacuated or in the armed forces? It touched the lives of everyone but was a different experience for all who lived through it.

7   Was there one particular person who influenced you more than any other?

8   Was there a turning point that changed your life?

9   What accomplishments can you recall with pride and pleasure?

10   Try to recall incidents or episodes in your life which were

amusing, unusual, frightening, triumphant and so on and which were of especial importance to you. Someone's death, perhaps, or a change in career direction; a crisis of some kind that forced a change in your life.

Beginnings

One doesn't become a writer by thinking about being a writer; one becomes a writer by writing.

P. D. James

I once asked a very successful novelist how one knew where to begin and met with a somewhat dismissive: 'At the beginning, of course,' which didn't answer my question at all. She, it seemed, had no trouble in finding the right place in which to open a story but, for many writers (including myself) it isn't always so simple.

Generally speaking, a novel should begin as close to a psychological turning point, and as near to some action, as possible. But even that can seem a bit vague when you're struggling to find the exact place to open. For instance, something has happened to set your main character (MC) on a different path so, do you begin by allowing us to see him or her facing whatever has occurred or plunge straight into the action and fill in the past in flashback? You may need to try several different ways, moving backwards and forwards in time, before you decide which is best. But, although a good opening is vital, you needn't worry too much at this stage, because many novelists are agreed that they usually have to go back and re-write the first chapter once the book is finished. In *The Rebecca Notebook* Daphne du Maurier tells how she came to write *Rebecca* and how what she had intended to be an epilogue somehow eventually merged into the first chapter so that both the beginning and ending changed from her original concept.

Nevertheless, you have to begin somewhere in order to get your book off the ground so let's take a look at some important points to bear in mind.

1   The opening must 'hook' the reader instantly, drawing him into the story. Most of us, browsing in bookshops and libraries are, first, either intrigued by the title (more about titles later), or have enjoyed other books by the same author. We then glance at the first page and, if that interests us sufficiently, we might look at the next two or three, flip through a few more and then decide whether to take it or put it back on the shelf. But it is on that initial page that everything rests. If our attention hasn't been caught by those first 350 words or so, we may look no further.

2   The main character must be introduced immediately and shown to be facing some kind of problem, actual or psychological.

3   Your opening must strike the keynote of the story: that is, let the reader know if it is a humorous novel, one of horror, adventure, romance and so on.

4   It should provide answers to some of the reader's questions: who and what is this person mentioned on page one who is obviously going to be the main character? Where and when is the story taking place? (The why, which is the most important question of all, can come later, probably by means of flashback.)

5   It should hint at coming conflict. This can be done in various ways. It can be overt, as in Diane Pearson's *Csardas* where the enchanting Ferenc sisters are allowed by their mother to go to a party unchaperoned because 'Papa won't be back for three weeks.' We know, instantly, that Papa is going to return early and that trouble lies ahead for the two sisters. It can be done more subtly, by suggesting a change in the weather, perhaps: a tiny cloud appearing in the halcyon sky, suggesting to the reader that a storm is brewing, metaphorically as well as in fact.

6   You should not introduce too many characters early on in your book. Establish your main characters first so that they become firmly fixed in the reader's mind.

7   Getting action going on the first page can be a useful ploy – that is, having something happen – but be wary of starting at too high a point or the interest may start sliding downwards instead of rising.

8   Opening with a line of dialogue is another way of grabbing the reader's attention. This is the opening of Catherine Cookson's *Katie Mulholland*.

> 'I don't like marriage, Mama.'
> 'You don't know what you're saying, child.'
> 'I do, mama, and I don't want to go back...I'm not going back.'

Now let's take a look at a few openings, chosen because I enjoyed them. One of my favourites is the gently ironic opening of *Daily & Sunday* by Richard Powell:

> Paul Wynnefield did not have a high opinion of the Chairman of the Board of Directors of the *Evening and Sunday Mail*. He was sorry about this, because he *was* the Chairman.

That left me wanting to know just why Paul Wynnefield didn't like himself.

> Today, Tuesday, the day that Penelope has chosen to leave her husband, is the first really warm day of spring.

From *Afternoon of a Good Woman* by Nina Bawden. Why is she leaving her husband and why on the first warm day of spring? My curiosity was instantly aroused.

> Has my watch stopped? No. But its hands do not seem to be going round. Don't look at them. Think of something else – anything else: think of yesterday, a calm, ordinary, easy-flowing day, in spite of the nervous tension of waiting.

21

From *The Woman Destroyed* by Simone de Beauvoir. Something awful has happened, clearly, but what?

> It is cold at six-forty in the morning of a March day in Paris and seems even colder when a man is about to be executed by firing squad. At that hour on 11th March 1963, in the main courtyard of the Fort d'Ivry, a French Air Force colonel stood before a stake driven into the chilly gravel as his hands were bound behind the post, and stared with slowly diminishing disbelief at the squad of soldiers facing him twenty metres away.

The Day of the Jackal by Frederick Forsyth. This opening is a good example of a piece of dramatic action literally dragging you into the story.

And, lastly, this opening from *Nile* by Laurie Devine:

> The day Um Mona dreaded dawned clear. Huddled on her haunches, she waited for them to come for her child.

How could anyone not want to read on after that?

In these beginnings, either something has already happened, or is about to happen, to the main character. They are each at a crossroad in their lives (or, in *The Day of the Jackal*, about to die though we don't yet know why). Curiosity to find out more will persuade the reader (the publisher's reader, in the first instance) to continue.

An alternative ploy to get your book 'off the ground' is to begin with an event *outside your main character's jurisdiction* that will set off a chain of causally-linked events which will inexorably lead to the climax of the novel.

Study the openings of novels you consider enjoyable and well-written, then put your own to the test. Ask yourself if it gives the reader sufficient information to cause him to become involved with, and curious about, your main character; if it sets the tone of the story about to be unfolded; if it hints at the coming conflict. If it does all these things, it's probably a good one, but bear in mind that you will need to re-assess it once you've completed your book.

Characterisation

Create your characters, give them a time and place to exist in, and leave the plot to them; the imposing of action on them is very difficult, since action must spring out of the temperament with which you have endowed them.

Anthony Burgess

That characters make your story is a truism. To test it, you only have to think back to those that have remained memorable for you. However original the plot, interesting the setting, it is the characters who spring instantly to mind. But in order for this to happen they first had to become real, living people to their creators.

A reason commonly given by publishers and editors for rejecting a work of fiction is that the characters were two-dimensional and unconvincing: 'cardboard cut-outs' or 'stereotypes'. This is almost certainly because they were not allowed a sufficiently long gestation period in the writer's mind before being committed to paper. Time spent thinking about a story, first, is always time well spent, partly, if not largely, because it will enable you to get to know these imaginary people, to 'round them out', know their foibles, their strengths and weaknesses, understand what will motivate them. It isn't until you are utterly familiar with them that you will be sure how they will react under the stress of the situation into which you will put them. And, if there is no stress to test them, there is no story to tell.

Names, physical description, speech, clothing all play a part in characterisation. Jason Ellis, tall, dark, bronzed and broad-shouldered with piercing cobalt blue eyes hooded by heavy lids, wears an open-necked shirt of cream silk, well-cut black trousers, Italian handmade leather shoes and a gold Cartier watch around his wrist. He seems the epitome of a romantic novel hero – successful, powerful and devastatingly attractive. To make him three-dimensional, however, he must have a human weakness, an inner vulnerability, or he will remain a stereotype. Maybe he has a jagged scar on his temple, the result of an accident when he was a child and which has left him, ever since, afraid of... Or he has been unable to trust a woman ever since his mother abandoned him when he was a child. But let's take a look at the various steps in creating believable characters, starting with names.

NAMES

Names carry definite connotations for most of us. Richard and John and David, for instance, are usually seen as 'nice guys' in fiction. Neville, Clive, Nigel and Gary are a bit suspect – 'smoothies', maybe. George is staid and dependable, as is Stanley or William. Mary is kind and motherly. Sal is probably a tomboy while Victoria or Lavinia are definitely upper-class.

Many writers attest that a story or novel won't work until they've found the right names for their characters.

Try to avoid giving main characters similar-sounding or same-initial names (it's surprisingly easy to fall into this trap): Maurice and Maureen; Wendy and William; Arnold and Barney.

DIALOGUE

This is one of the best ways of characterising. A. E. Coppard once said that a character does not come to life until he speaks and Peter Cheyney that you should let the reader find out about your character by the way he talks.

'I am afraid that I cannot allow James to participate in such a scheme.'

'No way is James going to do that.'

'I really don't think I can let James do that.'

These are three ways of saying the same thing but out of the mouths of very different people, one of whom is precise and pedantic, the second very much 'with it', using a currently fashionable idiom, while the third appears somewhat indecisive.

The language used will very much depend upon your characters' background and education. An uncouth sort of chap, tripping over an obstacle in the dark, will use far more 'colourful' words that a person of some refinement. So, if you don't like the idea of putting foul language into someone's mouth, you should not create someone like that.

Whilst clichés should be avoided in narrative, if your character is one who would talk and think in them, let him speak like that.

CLOTHING

This tells us a good deal about the person wearing it:

Harold Potterton's dog-tooth jacket would have been considered definitely trendy, ten years before. He wore it over a bright yellow polo-necked sweater; his feet were encased in cracked brown leather shoes with built-up heels and, on his head, a tweed cap tilted at a rakish angle over one eye.

PHYSICAL APPEARANCE

Tattoos on arm or chest; crimson-painted finger-nails; face devoid of make-up; bleached hair, all tell a little more, as do a character's expression and posture.

Harold's face settled back into its habitually-lugubrious expression as he slumped into his chair.

25

Millicent Arbuthnot and the straight-backed chair appeared to be part and parcel of each other.

MANNERISMS

Flicking an imaginary speck off a sleeve, straightening a cushion, meticulously re-arranging a flower or picture, running everywhere rather than walking; all these mannerisms will add to the picture you are trying to create.

With a novel, where you have so much more time to become thoroughly acquainted with your invented characters and whom you need to know in greater depth than for a short story, a device that can sometimes help is to keep a journal as if written by them: that way you'll really get inside them.

Your characters are likely to be a composite of people you have known in real life and, when you have put your character into a extreme situation where he will experience strong emotion, it is inevitable that part of yourself will also go into your creation. As writers we need to recognise that we are capable of feeling and doing anything that our characters do and feel, though normally we would not *actually* go to their extremes of anti-social behaviour. Is there anyone who has never told a lie, even if only a small one? Anyone who hasn't felt shame, deep anger or burning resentment?

Make sure, when creating a character, that you *show* the sort of person he is by description, dialogue and action rather than by making a subjective judgement about him. For example, don't tell us he is down at heel but let us see that for ourselves by the way he is portrayed.

Study some examples of characterisation in novels you've found memorable. In *Far From the Madding Crowd*, Thomas Hardy begins with a description of Gabriel Oak.

When Farmer Oak smiled, the corners of his mouth spread till they were within an unimportant distance of his ears, his eyes were reduced to chinks, and diverging wrinkles appeared round them, extending upon his countenance like the rays in a rudimentary sketch of the rising sun.

Doesn't this bring him instantly to life and tell us he is a pleasant, trustworthy man?

The following is from a story by H. E. Bates, *The Man Who Loved Squirrels*:

> Every day at noon his mother, a small, crisp, ferrety woman with hair like tangled sheep wool who always wore a pair of black old-fashioned high buttoned boots, brought his dinner up to him in a square brown wicker basket.

With a few deft brush-strokes, the writer has painted a vivid picture of the woman.

Many novelists write mini-biographies of their main characters before they begin. This can help avoid the sort of gaff where the heroine at the start of the book has blue eyes and half-way through they've changed to green. And when your characters become as real to you as members of your family, don't be surprised if they develop a life of their own. Most writers have experienced this and attest to a feeling of surprised and joyful incredulity when a character insists on behaving in a way contrary to how they (the author) intended. That's the moment when you know that you have breathed life into your character. And you can be sure, when that happens, that your book or story won't be rejected because of two-dimensional, 'cardboard' characters.

EXERCISE

Write a character sketch in about 500 words, possibly using someone you remember from childhood on which to build. Then put him/her into a situation which will test him/her to the limit. Hopefully, you'll end up with an idea for a short story – or maybe even a novel.

Children's fiction

I have to admit that I have never written for children: or rather, I did just once, many years ago. It was a little story entitled *The Adventures of Three Naughty Balloons*, was typed in single-spacing on octavo-size paper and sent out to a publisher of children's annuals. How 'green' we so often are when we first feel the itch to write and have little idea how to set about it professionally! Naturally, it was rejected – but...the following Christmas, my small daughter ran to me clutching a brightly illustrated annual, crying excitedly: 'Mummy, your story's here!' Sure enough, it was. At least, the incidents in it were exactly the same as in mine except that it was about only one balloon and not three.

The point of this tale is simply that it taught me a lesson. It taught me that, though I might have enough imagination to create stories, I had a lot to learn about writing, about structure and, not least, about presentation and the sooner I started learning, the quicker I would be likely to succeed.

From here on, I can only pass on to you some points I have learned about this very demanding type of writing from observation, from reading and from listening and talking to experts in the field. The first five points concern basic considerations in writing for children; points 6 to 12 are practical hints on how to make your work saleable.

1   Children's fiction should not be seen as an easy option. It isn't. Young children are critical beings with few inhibitions about stating their likes and dislikes and a built-in knack of spotting insincerity. As with any type of writing, you should only attempt it because you genuinely want to do it and not solely because of any money you hope will come rolling in. After all, why waste time and energy on something that your heart and soul are not in?

2   Write for the child that is within you. Many of the best children's writers have affirmed this. A story written with this motivation will remain popular, however limited to a certain time and class. I think of my children's copy of C.S. Lewis's *The Lion, the Witch and the Wardrobe*, which had almost disintegrated by the time they outgrew it. The book is as much in demand now as it was a generation ago.

3   If you are writing a story set in the 1980s write for the child who lives in a multi-racial, multi-cultural society, may well belong to a one-parent family and have grown up believing this is to be the norm. Remember that customs within our society have changed enormously over the past few decades. Fathers bathe their babies, change their nappies, carry them in slings against their chests and, in general, play a much more active and intimate role in their upbringing, no longer being seen mainly as authoritarian figures.

Beware of writing from the standpoint of your own childhood, of basing your story on nostalgia for your own. And remember that boarding-schools and feasts in the dorm are definitely 'out'.

Hilda Thomas's novel *The Runaways*, which won the 1988 Guardian Children's Fiction Award, drew upon her experiences as a teacher in a city multi-racial school.

4   We are now, thankfully, in an age where sexual discrimination is frowned upon, so help further this by avoiding sexism and role-stereotyping. In a story aimed at a readership of boys and girls, make your main character a girl, for a change, and let her take a leading, active role in the adventure you are relating. One successful children's writer has suggested that lively, enterprising girl heroines are what are needed in today's stories, like Jo, the strong, tomboyish character in *Little Women*.

5   Never write 'down' to your potential reader. Children deserve to be treated with respect. (Remember it is the child in you you're writing for.)

6   You must keep your eyes on market trends and you can do this by reading the latest children's fiction, especially those books which have won awards or which your librarian tells you are proving popular. Browse in bookshops and libraries, talk to booksellers and librarians, write to publishers for their catalogues, read children's papers if you want to try short stories for them. Whilst the latter might not pay much for any work they accept, they will help you learn your craft and teach you which topics are popular and which are not. For instance, at the present moment, witches (especially naughty ones) are 'in'. Dinosaurs are perennial favourites, as are furry animals, while dragons appear to be on the way out – fairies and pixies most definitely are.

I hear some of you protesting that your children or grandchildren just adore your invented fairytales and are always clamouring for more. Well, that may be true but you must bear in mind that they know you, the storyteller, which greatly enhances the tales for them. Would a group of unknown children be equally enthralled? Also, rightly or wrongly, publishers believe they have their finger on the pulse of market requirements and, to a large extent, the children's fiction available is dictated by what adults (parents, teachers, librarians and publishers) believe is wanted.

7   Stories for children should reflect some aspects of social learning: in other words, have an underlying theme, a tiny, implicit 'message'. One such might be that, having run away and met with various adventures, a seven-year-old 'comes to realise' that home really is the best place to be, after all, with his toys, his teddy bear and icecream for tea.

8   Keep your plots simple though with plenty of action and excitement. At a time when Enid Blyton was frowned upon by educationalists, I remember again my daughter's comment on *The Secret Seven*: 'Something's always happening, Mum' (said with a sigh of satisfaction). And if Enid Blyton was responsible for her becoming a prolific reader, that can't be bad, surely?

·9 Use plenty of dialogue, 50 per cent at least. This not only serves to increase the pace but it is easier for the child to absorb than large chunks of narrative.

10 Make your main character a normal child who isn't too good to be true. This will aid reader-identification, which is one of the secrets of all good story-telling.

11 Plot your story first and ensure your main character has a problem to solve or a goal to achieve (buying Mum a birth-day present, for example). Place obstacles, boulders even, in the way so as to create conflict and make sure the resolution comes about through the main character's ingenuity and not by some adult coming to the rescue. In fact, it's wise to get any adults off the scene fairly quickly, leaving the stage to the children.

12 As with all fiction, the ending of a story should be a satisfying one, leaving the main character having learned some-thing, having gone through some psychological change, having grown up a little.

13 Before putting pen to paper, you need to decide on your readership: up to 7; 7-9; 9-13 and 13-plus (the teenage or young adult sector) are the usually applied age-groupings.

This is a vital consideration: your characters, the vocabulary, the storyline and its structure will differ for each age group. For instance, with stories for very young children, repetition is essential. Think for instance of *The Three Billy-goats Gruff* or *Goldilocks and the Three Bears*, where each piece of action occurs thrice.

It would also be wise to have some idea of the sort of story that is especially popular with your chosen age-group, which means doing some market study. For example, Roald Dahl's books are high on the list of favourites for 9- to 13-year-olds (according to librarians, booksellers and children alike) yet are macabre, often quite horrific and might be seen as being totally unsuitable for children. However, as one librarian explained, there is often a very fine line between what is acceptable and what is not (in adult eyes, at least). And a blend of fantasy and reality never seems to go out of fashion.

Books for the children's section of libraries are generally chosen by panels of educationalists. Adults also decide on which books should win an award. This being so, you should find it helpful to study those books considered to be the best – as a guide only for your own writing and not, of course, to imitate. Four authors whom librarians find popular and whose books are considered to be of a high standard, as well as those mentioned above, are: Penelope Lively, Nina Bawden, Dick King-Smith, and Philippa Pearce.

There are several series of books published, aimed roughly at the 7-9 age-group, which you might think worth studying if that is the age you are interested in writing for: Banana Books (Heinemann); Toppers (Deutsch); Gazelle (Hamish Hamilton); Hopscotch (Hodder & Stoughton).

There are many others aimed at those just beginning to read, as well as at those who are read to, most of which contain a high proportion of illustrations. The majority of publishers choose their own artists and are not interested in seeing illustrations accompanying a typescript. However, if you are able to provide illustrations of a professional quality, there is no harm in mentioning this and perhaps enclosing a few examples.

Top Tip from Tessa Krailing

Author of *How to Write for Children* (Allison & Busby, 1988).

If I had to put my finger on the single most important quality that every good writer of children's fiction must possess, it would be – perhaps surprisingly – energy. By that I mean the indefinable quality that gives your work driving power and lifts it head and shoulders above the mundane, the trivial, the all-too-predictable type of children's story. It doesn't matter how few words you use to tell your tale: creative energy will shine through even the shortest paragraph. But it's the 'something extra' you need to make a publisher sit up and take notice when your book lands on his or her desk – and to ensure that children not only read your book but also remember it for years to come.

Confessions, or true-life stories

The success of this type of story lies in its immediacy, its intimacy, its sense of someone confiding in you, and you alone, their guilty secret or the awful situation they're in. I mean, how could you possibly resist listening with both ears when a friend is spilling out the dreadful thing she's done (it's usually a 'she' though not always) or is contemplating doing?

'Sin, suffer and repent' is the term once used in connection with these stories and, whilst it is still true of some of them, it no longer describes them all. But there is always a moral, lesson or basic truth implied at the end: they are modern morality tales and, especially important for the teenage market, can get over a 'message' without preaching, which would not be acceptable to young people today.

For instance, because I felt concerned about how young girls often seem to crave a ring on the third finger of their left hand and refuse to listen to advice that they are far too young to be thinking of marriage, I wrote a 'Reader's True Experience' (RTE) about such a girl. It opened with 'me' having a blazing row with my parents just before my boyfriend comes round to discuss getting married. In fact, I have forced him into the situation. He arrives late and, when I open the door to him, he bursts into tears and blurts out that he's lost his job. Unable to cope with the turn of events, I allow myself to be pushed into another room and let my mother comfort the boy. Thus, 'I' come to realise that my parents are right and that we are not ready for the responsibilities and difficulties of marriage.

I hope that maybe it helped some girl, somewhere, to become a little more mature and realistic.

Unfortunately, too often, these stories are sneered at by those who haven't tried to write them or taken the trouble to study them. This is a pity because they are an excellent training ground for writing in the first person and for getting emotion into your fiction. And, if you can't move your readers to laughter or tears, make them empathise, make them feel compassion, joy, anger or horror, even, you have failed as a writer of any kind of fiction.

All fictional characters must have a flaw in order to be believable and it is this flaw which is the springboard for the 'true' story. Maybe they have a jealous disposition; are inclined to extravagance; tend to be over-submissive: it is this weakness in their nature that gets them into the difficult situation around which the story revolves. It doesn't have have to be an extremely dramatic situation but it must be one of conflict. Even where the protagonist is passive, the one suffering because of another's behaviour, the 'flaw' and the resulting conflict are still hers.

Suppose, for instance, your main character is married to an alcoholic who hits her. Her character flaw is likely to be cowardice or being too submissive. She is in a terrible situation, albeit not of her own making, but it is a continuing one because she is afraid to do anything about it. Whilst one is not minimising her difficulties, nevertheless, both in life and in fiction, nothing will change unless she makes it change. In fiction, as in life, something important must be at stake to force her into action. So, let's take a look at the battered wife idea and see how we can make a story out of it that perhaps will make the reader shed a tear but also give a little sigh of relief and satisfaction at the end.

First, what do we know of our MC and her life? And what point is she at? Remember that 'crisis' means 'decision' and that to motivate her into decisive action something vital must be at stake. Now we come to the 'suppose that?' 'what if?' part of planning a story. What if she has been married for five years to a macho sort of man, handsome but domineering? Before they were married, he had hit her occasionally, but she hadn't been too worried, believing he would soften once they were together for always. Only he hasn't done so, and the fact that she hasn't become pregnant seems to enrage him. Fertility tests have proved that the fault is not hers and she remembers the day when she timidly suggested that he, too, should go for tests and he knocked her to the ground and kicked her for daring to

35

question his virility. He accused her of being less than a woman for failing to conceive, taunting her and comparing her with other women he's slept with.

We now learn how desperately she wants a child, partly to satisfy her own maternal longings but partly to appease her husband and prove she is all-woman. She fears she might lose him otherwise.

That, of course, would solve the problem of her being a battered wife but wouldn't make a satisfying story: she must resolve the conflict *by her own efforts*.

But first things first: where to begin? To set the scene, show her problem and the frightening situation she is in, the best opening would probably be a piece of action where her husband is actually physically ill-treating her, as well as jeering at her non-fertility. The reader will be in no doubt as to her predicament.

Next, in a flashback (a frequently used device in this kind of fiction) we can learn that, as a child, our MC frequently watched her father hitting her mother, and that he had often taken a belt to her too. It is a well-known psychological phenomenon that people repeat patterns, and she has grown up conditioned to wives being beaten by husbands, though vowing she will never let a child of hers be subjected to the same sort of treatment. Here we are given a clue as to the climax of the story – the 'blackest moment' which will make her finally take action.

Moving back to the present, we see her go to the doctor's where she learns that, at last, she is pregnant. She is overjoyed; all her troubles are ended because her husband will now love and cherish her as he vowed to do during their wedding ceremony. She hurries home to cook a special meal, puts on a pretty dress, places a lighted candle on the table and waits to greet him with the wonderful news. Her heart sinks as he comes in from work and she sees his bad temper, which is worsened by her elaborate romantic preparations. As he lifts his hand to strike her she blurts out her news, certain it will stop him. It does, for half a second, and then his fist smashes into her face as he knocks her to the ground. 'So what?' he snarls. 'A proper woman would've been years ago. And there'd better be no saying you're sick and no baby wailing while I'm around, I'm telling you now.'

His foot comes up to launch a kick, she curls herself into a ball to protect her stomach and rolls out of reach. She gets up and faces him angrily and, astonished and shame-faced, he turns and flings out of the house. We see her blow out the candle and sit silently weeping in the darkness for a while, then get up, go into her bedroom and pack a small suitcase with a few things. She has finally accepted that her husband will never change but that she can, and must, for the sake of her coming baby. Life won't be easy, she knows, but at least she will have someone to love and who will love her. And, despite her sadness and fear, she walks out of the house and down the street with a firm tread: she has, at last, arrived at a resolution.

I've spent some time in showing how this type of story is built up from its opening to its crisis and resolution in the hope that it will encourage you to try to write one. It is unquestionably the largest market for the short story today. Although the majority have women protagonists, each issue of a magazine usually carries one told from a male viewpoint.

Many of the problems dealt with are of the 'human interest' type dealing with family relationships, problems in a work situation, and so on. Some have a contemporary focus, and may involve drug-taking, alcoholism, tug-of-love children or baby-snatching. Certain once-taboo subjects, such as child abuse and incest, can now be used if handled with care.

You will probably read some which seem to aim at sexual titillation but many strike a much deeper note, are warmly and sensitively written and have given the writer the added satisfaction of hoping they may have genuinely shed some light on, and suggested a way out of, an apparently insoluble dilemma that someone, somewhere, is trying to cope with.

Different magazines publish a selection of different types of story: a tear-jerker, a tender romance, a warm, human-interest story, an action-packed one, a supernatural or mystery story, perhaps. There is usually a fairly wide scope. Study the particular magazine you think you could write for to see what kind it takes. Look at the ages of the main characters, whether they are mostly married or single, their jobs and backgrounds, whether the stories are from the male viewpoint.

37

Finally, a summary of practical considerations:

1   Remember that reader-identification is all-important. At the end, the reader should think: 'There, but for the Grace of God, go I.'

2   Use plenty of dialogue to provide pace and movement.

3   Start at a high-point in the story and provide information as to motivation in dramatised flashbacks.

4   Use shortish sentences.

Don't forget that most 'true-life' stories don't have a by-line (that is, the name of the author doesn't appear) because they purport to be true and so, clearly, the narrator wishes to remain anonymous: indeed, to give a by-line would tend to suspend belief rather than the opposite.

MARKETS

Many magazines take this type of story, from teenage ones such as *Jackie, Patches* and *Blue Jeans* (D.C. Thomson) to *Loving* (IPC) and those published by Argus (*True Romances, True Story, Woman's Story* and *Love Story*) Atlantic Publishing Company (*My Story* and *Romance*).

It is up to you to study them and send for their guidelines. In the main, their readers are not highly educated, probably work in shops, offices or factories, or did so before marriage, and may well be unemployed. They are likely to live in a provincial town, often in the Midlands or North of England. And, lastly, remember that the 'I' is likely to be a little bit bolder than the reader herself would be.

Conflict

Conflict is the stuff of drama: without it, there is no story, no play. It has been described as the fuel that keeps a story moving. Like a car without petrol, a story without conflict won't go anywhere, but the word often gives rise to misunderstanding in the minds of beginner-writers.

My dictionary defines it thus: 'a fight, a struggle, a contest; opposition of interests, opinions or purpose; mental strife.' It does not state that it must, of necessity, involve physical violence or even verbal sparring. What it does always involve, however, is a struggle of some kind between two factors: man against man (external); man against himself (internal); man against nature (external).

A student of mine once protested that she didn't like conflict in her own life, didn't want to write about it and failed to see why I was insisting it was necessary in her story. I countered by asking which was her favourite book. Without hesitation, she replied: Winston Graham's *Demelza*. I pointed out that that story is full of conflict between the different social classes of eighteenth-century Cornwall, between the people and the mines dug deep into the earth, and between individuals. She had failed to grasp the concept of conflict as it relates to fiction.

It is only through conflict that your characters reveal themselves, show their hidden depths, their strengths and weaknesses. Of necessity, conflict will accompany their problems and their problems will stem from their attitudes and backgrounds.

Foreshadowing is an excellent way of heightening its impact. For example, in John le Carré's *A Perfect Spy*, Magnus Pym reads out a passage from the Bible in which Judas betrays Christ. A short while later in the book, Magnus himself betrays a friend. The betrayal has been foreshadowed.

Conflict is about opposing forces and should be present in every major scene. Often, a beginner will duck out at the last moment, pull up short and avoid the conflict between or within characters that has been promised, thus weakening his story and irritating the reader, who feels cheated of his expectations.

Put at is simplest, conflict involves someone wanting something and facing obstacles, internal or external, which prevent this goal being attained. Give your main character a goal that is vital to their well-being, place one or more obstacles in their path, turn the screw as often as you realistically can without straining credibility and you'll have written a novel, short story or play that might have many flaws but which will stand the ultimate test – it will keep your reader or audience to the end.

Contracts

Whilst at this stage of the game the question of contracts is not likely to be of much significance to you, it would seem appropriate to mention one or two points to bear in mind for the future when you become successful.

Although contracts vary from publisher to publisher, the Society of Authors and the Writers' Guild of Great Britain have produced a Minimum Terms Agreement (known as MTA) which a number of publishers have accepted as being fair to everyone. There is an excellent book on the subject entitled *Publishing Agreements: A Book of Precedents* by Charles Clark, published in 1984 by Allen & Unwin. It is relatively expensive to buy but should be in your local library and would be worth reading if and when you come to the point of submitting a novel to a publisher.

The contract will state what you, the author, will be paid as an advance against the royalties you will earn – if the book sells! – and will include numerous other clauses. For example, one will protect the publisher from unnecessary expense should you refuse to undertake certain agreed revisions of the text. It may also contain an option clause by which you promise to give him the first refusal on your next book (and sometimes the next two). You don't have to agree to this or, indeed, to any of the clauses in the contract you are offered; but you can only change them with the publisher's full understanding and prior consent. Remember that the contract is as much for the publisher's protection as yours, and the wording of the contract is designed to be in the mutual interest of both parties.

In 1982 the Publisher's Association laid down a Code of Practice containing a set of principles recommended for use in dealings between publishers and authors. This is set out in *Publishing Agreements: A Book of Precedents* and makes interesting reading, stipulating as it does 'that the publisher must recognise the importance of co-operation with an author in an enterprise to which both are essential. This relationship can be fulfilled only in an atmosphere of confidence, in which authors get the fullest possible credit for their work and achievements.' This must surely be reassuring for all writers, whether published or aspiring.

Copyright

This is a subject that bothers many beginning writers and is undoubtedly a complex one in its entirety, as covered by the Copyright Act of 1956. However, for most purposes it can be narrowed down to more comprehensible proportions.

Basically, the words you have written, be it a letter to a friend or a novel or a play, remain yours. Legally, this means that no one can reproduce them, either in full or in substantial part, without your permission. There is no need to do anything to demonstrate that they belong to you, not even by putting © on the cover-sheet of your typescript: you have written them and that is sufficient. However, there are corollaries. If you have agreed to part with your copyright, for whatever reason, that is an end to it so far as you are concerned. Also, once you have entered into a contract with a publisher, he will have certain rights. In return for royalties, he has been licensed to reprint your book at any time during an agreed specified period if he so wishes and until he renounces those rights. This period used to be for as long as fifty years after the author's death (and, in some cases, still is) but is often for twenty-five years. Under the Minimum Terms Agreement (drawn up by The Society of Authors and the Writers' Guild of Great Britain and operated by a growing number of publishers), it is suggested that the licence should be for ten years only, covering the average two/three years' lifespan for a hardback edition plus seven/eight years for a paperback. Clearly this is negotiable between publisher and author. The Society of Authors produces a *Quick Guide to Publishing Contracts* which it might be useful to consult, if in doubt.

Copyright laws also protect work for fifty years after the death of an author so that if, for example, you become famous and your writings of extreme value, no one can reproduce them until

43

fifty years have elapsed after your demise without the permission of whoever inherited them. With regard to letters, note that, whilst the actual paper on which they were written belongs to the recipient, the words themselves still belong to the writer.

It is useful to remember that there is no copyright in facts, titles, ideas or even skeleton plots. Often enough it seems that ideas float around in the ether and that more than one writer reaches up to grab them so that extraordinarily similar stories appear in print at around the same time. Two of my students in two entirely separate groups read out stories in which an elderly man discovered, to his annoyance, a young girl trespassing in what he considered to be his own private piece of countryside. Had they belonged to the same group, there might well have been some ill-feeling over this coincidence.

The same law applies to photographs and drawings, so if you submit an article with illustrations which are not your own work, you must first obtain the written permission of the photographer, artist, or the owner of the copyright, which might be an institution such as the British Museum. It is unlikely they will refuse, provided they receive acknowledgement in the article, but will probably ask for a fee. You might then, in the case of an article, come to an agreement whereby you will pass on to them whatever portion you receive for illustrations from the publisher, asking for this to be noted separately.

There is a golden rule which every writer should bear in mind and that is: never part with your copyright. The only exception to this is if it is a short piece and you think it unlikely you will ever sell it anywhere else. That being the case, you may decide it is preferable to have one fee for it, at least, and not be unduly worried if that is the last of it. For a larger work, however, such as a book, play, or short story, it is unwise to sign away your copyright. As regards a short story, you might be able to sell it abroad and so double its earnings for you. No reputable publisher would ask for copyright, anyway, but a few magazines do, on occasion, sending you a brief form of contract for your signature. I have one before me, now, which states: ALL COPYRIGHT FOR ALL PURPOSES. You are at liberty, if you wish, to cross out those words and sign the deletion, replacing them with FIRST BRITISH SERIAL RIGHTS, which is what is normally offered (see below).

As a beginner-writer you are likely to be concerned with articles and short stories only, in which case you should type at the foot of the cover-sheet of their typescript the words FIRST BRITISH SERIAL RIGHTS, or simply FBSR. If you forget, though, it isn't disastrous because, by implication, that is what you are offering; you are allowing the magazine or newspaper to publish this piece of work for the first time in Britain. (This has nothing to do with serialisation of your work.) If, later, you decide to try and sell the piece again, you must state that you are offering Second British Serial Rights, in which case the editor will want to know where and when it previously appeared. National periodicals are not generally interested in something another has already used. (Naturally, this does not mean that you can't use the same information, facts and figures in a completely rewritten piece, giving it another slant for a different type of market.) However, where localised markets are concerned, there is a rough one hundred mile radius beyond which it is possible that another editor might be interested. For instance, if you sold a piece on, say, Guy Fawkes' Day to the *Exeter Express*, offering FBSR, you could also try a paper in Yorkshire offering Second Rights, explaining in a covering letter where it will also appear.

When it comes to material for the BBC, you will receive a contract spelling out exactly what rights the Company requires. The right to an option for repeats is usual and, if a repeat broadcast is made, you will receive an additional fee.

An important point to bear in mind is that, if you wish to reproduce words written by someone else, there is a convention (referred to as 'fair dealing' in the 1956 Copyright Act) which allows for short extracts of copyright material to be reprinted free of charge for purposes of criticism and review, as long as the extract is less than four hundred words (and it would be wise to use far less) or not more than one quarter of the total work. As regards poetry, it should not be more than forty lines or more than one quarter of a complete poem. This convention was arrived at by The Society of Authors and the Publishers'

Association jointly. However, you should always seek the permission of the copyright holder before you use the piece in question. (For further clarification consult *A Handbook of Copyright in British Publishing Practice*, published by Cassell, revised edition, 1984.)

Incidentally, copyright laws in the USA differ from those in Britain.

Another question which often seems to worry new writers is how to protect their work from being stolen. If you have written, and submitted to a television company, a play or a pilot script for a highly original TV situation comedy series, you might, understandably, wish to ensure that no one else could possibly get hold of it and pass it off as their own work. One way to prevent this is to send a copy to yourself by registered post, then deposit it in a bank, unopened, which would be proof, if it were ever needed in a court of law, that it had been written by you at a certain date. Another method is simply to lodge a copy with your bank in a sealed envelope. However, such measures are, on the whole, unnecessary and you should not become neurotic about literary theft (see Plagiarism, p. 98).

To sum up:

1   Whatever you have written is protected by the laws of copyright until fifty years after your death, unless you have signed away that right.

2   Think carefully about selling your copyright for anything but short articles.

3   You may use a short extract of prose or poetry for the purposes of criticism or review so long as you make acknowledgement in your text and acquire the necessary permissions first.

4   You must obtain permission to use any illustrations that are not your own work, and pay the necessary fees.

5   There is no copyright in facts, titles, ideas or basic plots.

If you are researching into a subject, any facts you come across are yours for the taking but you must write them into your text in your own words and not someone else's.

6   Do not be worried that someone might steal your work: it's unlikely to happen.

Description

The description of a place, a setting, a character, even an object, should be an integral part of a work of fiction, serving a definite purpose. For instance, descriptions of place, however lyrical, should not seem to be lifted out of a travelogue. As demonstrated by the extracts below, they can be used effectively to heighten emotion, either observed through the eyes of the main character and related to his/her mood or linked to the tone and action of the story, perhaps as an indicator of what is going to happen.

And descriptions should be vivid enough to produce a physical and/or emotional response in the reader. For instance, a description of small white teeth biting into a ripe peach, its juice spurting down the chin, should almost make him salivate.

This is where skill comes in: where the selectivity and discrimination urged by Henry James should be employed. A beginner tends to describe a scene or a character in the first words that spring to mind, and often in considerable detail. But, just as a painter doesn't cram everything he sees into his picture but chooses to emphasise and highlight his own perception of what is before him, so the writer should do the same. Painter and writer (and what is a writer but a painter with words?) are creating illusions of reality, not reality itself. Each sets out to deliberately manipulate the emotions, to create a sense of place, by the various means at his disposal: by use of technique.

Evoking a response in the reader will depend on the judicious use of adjectives, strong verbs and on associations. Suppose, for example, you need a scene in which a door looms large, the description of that door will be crucial to how the reader perceives that section of your story. If it is of solid dark oak with ornate carvings of vine-leaves, bunches of grapes and wine-goblets and is firmly locked, it might well suggest that the character struggling to open it is also trying to open up and enrich his life in some way. The door then becomes symbolic and will stand quite a lengthy description in which all five senses might be employed. Maybe your character bangs his fist against it and feels its hard resistance; presses his face to it and becomes aware of a certain smell emanating from it. Perhaps he puts his ear against it to catch a faint sound from behind.

Here is a descriptive passage taken from Penelope Lively's *The Road to Lichfield*.

> Ten years ago...she used to bring the children down here on afternoon walks, when they were three and five. To walk this lane now was to feel again their small hands cling to hers as they darted back from private sorties to the ditch, the five-barred gate to the field, the arthritic branches of the willow at the corner. Passing the Span houses, she had caught herself in an automatic glance to see if the ditch was flooded, a possible child-hazard. But the Span houses had not been built then; there had been a field of cows where they stood and the ditch was drained and tamed now, nothing but a sulky lair for nettles and docks. Splatt's cottage had seemed, then, entirely different, a faintly mysterious place, the beckoning climax of a walk...a Hansel and Gretel house in the woods.

Surely, possible hazards to herself are in her mind at that moment, suggested by the 'sulky lair for nettles' and the 'Hansel and Gretel house'.

Here is a descriptive passage used to quite different ends, from Joseph Kessel's *The Lion*.

> But already, during that brief interlude, the tropical dawn – an amazingly short-lived phenomenon – had passed into morning. Out of the heart of darkness light suddenly sprang, gloriously arrayed, darting shafts of splendour. The whole world broke into brilliant, sparkling iridescence; crimson arrows streaked across the snows of Kilimanjaro.
>
> The sunlight melted the mist away, breaking it up into tattered wisps and wreaths and spirals of steamy air which,

in their turn, condensed into heavy dew, all spangled and twinkling like crushed diamonds.

Something exceptional is surely about to occur?

EXERCISE

Take an object or place that has some significance to you, a symbolic significance, perhaps, such as a particular door, a garden, an attic, a doll – anything that conjures up for you particular associations – and describe it so that someone reading it will react strongly to it. Don't stop at just a few paragraphs of pure description but carry on and see where it leads you. You might be surprised and go on to write a story or even a novel.

Dialogue

Good dialogue in fiction is vitally important, be it intended to be read or listened to. It has certain specific functions to perform and should never be included unless it is performing these functions, which are:

to reveal character and background;
to impart necessary information;
to move the story forward.

It should create the impression of real speech although, in fact, it won't be natural. It will be more like edited speech. If you listen attentively to someone talking, you will quickly realise how ineffective it would be to transpose all those words into written dialogue, with their 'ums' and 'ers', interruptions and asides. If you want to test this for yourself, tape-record a conversation with a friend, then play it back and imagine listening to it in a play. You'll quickly realise how impossible it would be.

There is no better way of learning how to write effective dialogue than by listening to radio plays (and reading them, too, because many of the best are available in book form). Speaking your dialogue aloud will help you hear if it sounds right and, if you are writing a play, using a tape-recorder to play it back is invaluable.

Become an eavesdropper, listening to conversations in cafés or on buses and listen attentively to speech patterns. Not only will your ear become attuned, you'll probably be bombarded with ideas for plots and be vastly entertained, also. Try it and see.

Now let us consider the specific functions of dialogue.

REVEALING CHARACTER AND BACKGROUND

A. E. Coppard said that a character does not come to life until he speaks. Peter Cheyney's advice was that you should let the reader find out about your character by the way he talks. To give a very simple example, if a navvy drops a hammer on his foot, he isn't going to say: 'Oh dear!' His language is likely to be a string of expletives to which an editor or reader might well object. However, if your story or play involves such a character, then it is unlikely you will be able to avoid strong language, except possibly by the occasional use of a row of points, e.g. f... or b... If this character is central to your story, you will have to find alternative ways of characterising.

Regional speech patterns and phraseology such as catch-phrases and verbal mannerisms can be an effective way of bringing a character to life because they are so recognisable and evocative. A simple example: if someone says 'Top 'o the mornin' to you' there's no need to state that he's from Southern Ireland because that particular phrase has virtually become a cliché for an Irishman. The use of 'any road...' suggests a northerner. 'There's terrible isn't it?' or 'It's proud of you I am' and you can almost hear a lilting Welsh voice speaking the words. No other nationality would juxtapose them in that way.

Dialect, though, is more tricky and, unless you are very familiar with it should be used sparingly. To suggest Devonshire speech, for instance, dropping in the occasional 'm' dear' would probably be sufficient.

Dialogue can be used to indicate personal characteristics, but with discretion. Suppose you have a verbose character, the sort of woman who never stops talking and who waylays people in the street. You cannot possibly give her great long speeches to show us that. You must suggest it more subtly. For instance: 'Oh, there you are, Mrs Brown. I knew I'd see you, this morning. I said as much to my husband. I said...' Then go on to have Mrs Brown mentally switching off her hearing while keeping her smile fixed on her lips and thinking, 'Stupid old bore. If it wasn't for her husband on the Council, I'd tell her to get lost.'

In this way the reader learns something about both women.

Dialogue can also indicate mood. If angry, a person is likely to speak in a rapid burst of speech; if nervous, in short, hesitant snatches.

Characterisation through dialogue, well handled, can obviate the need to insert 'Molly said' 'Jim remarked' 'Mark commented', etc. That isn't to say you should leave such tags out entirely (it can lead to confusion), but do so wherever possible. In a radio play called *The Teddy Bear's Picnic* in which a couple of American robot toys attempt a take-over of an English boy's toy cupboard, there was no question about who was talking to whom when one character spoke the following lines: 'How long you been here? Ain't that your tummy hanging out? Ain't that a shame.' The teddy bear spoke very differently, in ultra-English, very precisely: 'I think this is a very poor show.' A little exaggerated, perhaps, but extremely effective in creating instantly recognisable characters for radio.

In connection with dialogue, there is one basic mistake that is often made, especially by older people who experienced a thoroughly prescriptive approach to grammar at school, and that is that they avoid using contractions even though they would when talking. The spoken forms 'I won't', 'I can't', 'I shouldn't', become 'I will not', 'I cannot', 'I should not'. Only if the character you are portraying would actually speak in this way are you using dialogue correctly. Otherwise you should use the contractions. For example, perhaps an elderly ex-schoolteacher would say: 'I will not be able to attend your party this evening', whilst most of us would say: 'I won't be able to come to your party tonight.' If you know you have a tendency to write in an unnaturally formal manner, make a note to check on your dialogue after you have written your story.

Similarly, if your character is not highly educated, let him/her speak ungrammatically, e.g. 'I'm just going to have a lay down on the bed.' 'It weren't me that done it.' There is no need to explain that he/she only had basic schooling,

53

we know from the dialogue. This leads to dialogue's second function.

IMPARTING INFORMATION

Providing necessary information is a valuable function of dialogue but it must not be done in an artificial manner. For instance, if the reader needs to know that Sandra has just received an invitation to a wedding and that the groom is her ex-fiancé with whom she is still in love, we mustn't learn in this unsubtle way:

> 'Oh no,' Sandra cried in a choked whisper, tearing open the envelope and gazing at the shiny white card inside. 'How could John send me an invitation to his wedding so soon after he broke our engagement?'

Instead, say something like:

> Sandra tore open the envelope and gazed numbly at the shiny white card in her hand. 'Oh no,' she cried aloud in a choked whisper, 'how could you?' She turned to Joanna. 'It's an invitation to a wedding,' she murmured brokenly. 'John's wedding.' And her eyes strayed to the third finger of her left hand where a narrow white band contrasted starkly with the rest of her skin.

We then don't need to be told that Sandra has recently been engaged to John, that he is about to be married to someone else and that she is still in love with him.

Often, someone new to writing, having been told that dialogue helps to break up chunks of narrative on a page, will pepper their script with social chit-chat.

> Mary James closed her front door and was hurrying down the path when she spied her neighbour in the next garden. 'Good morning, Mrs Thomson,' she chirped. 'It's a lovely day, isn't it? About time, too, after all that rain.'

This conversation might continue for several lines, none of it relevant to the storyline. Even if the fact that it's been raining recently is a vital clue to something that is about to happen, the neighbour should not be introduced merely to provide this information. Another way would be more appropriate.

Suppose it is important to know that a certain character has a drink problem which he is either trying to conquer or to hide. If, at a party, he refuses an alcoholic drink, saying he'd rather have an orange juice, and someone remarks sardonically: 'What's up with you, then? Gone on the wagon?' we know his behaviour is unusual and make a mental note that there must be a good reason for it which we will find out later. Unless the remark was of significance in this way then it ought not to have been put in.

MOVING THE STORY FORWARD

Martha and her young cousin, Gerald, have just arrived in a small town in a remote part of Crete. We haven't yet learned why but suspect it will have a bearing on the plot.

> Gerald turned from the window and regarded Martha balefully. 'What are we going to do here? Looks a bit of a dump to me.'
> Martha flashed him a hesitant glance. 'Well, I think we'd better unpack, first, don't you? Then,' she went on casually, 'I thought we might try to find the Villa Minos. I've heard it's...very interesting.'

We now know that the Villa is going to play an important part in the story but that Martha doesn't want her cousin to know why, for the moment, at any rate.

I hope the following extract will demonstrate various functions of dialogue: how it breaks up a page, making it easier on the eye; characterises; provides some information and moves the story forward. Note also how it should be set out. You should indent (that is, begin a new paragraph) whenever a character speaks afresh and enclose everything that is spoken, including punctuation, in single quotation marks (reserving double for reported speech).

55

'Dearest,' he said, 'dearest, allow me to know what is best for both of us. We will go together to...'

'But James,' Angela broke in, 'how can you possibly know what's best for me? I hardly know myself but at least I'm willing to discuss it.' She lifted her chin and stared defiantly at him, the man to whom she had become engaged only a few hours before. And, for the first time since she'd known him, a doubt crept into her mind.

'Angela, this really will not do.' James jerked an impatient shoulder. 'I must insist that you do not interrupt me when I am speaking. Now, let me continue. As I said, we will go together to see your grandfather and...'

'No, James,' Angela burst in once more. 'I couldn't bear to go there again. Not now. Don't you remember what he said to me? "Disobey me, Angela, and I shall never, I repeat never, allow you inside my home again." Please, James, if you truly love me, you won't try to make me.'

A long drawn-out sigh escaped James's lips. 'Oh, very well, my love. But I do not understand you. And I do wonder...' Then it was his turn to break off mid-sentence.

'Yes?' Angela's head had shot up and green eyes glinted with incipient anger.

Interspersing dialogue with short pieces of action (e.g. 'a sigh escaped James's lips'; 'Angela's head had shot up') helps to pull the reader back into the scene, also moving the story on a little and stimulating the senses. Another example of this:

'So I think we should definitely leave tomorrow, Ettie. I'll set the alarm for seven...' As Mavis's voice clattered on, Ettie was aware of the heavy scent of lilacs drifting in through the open window and, suddenly, she was two hundred miles away in...

EXERCISE

Practise characterising through dialogue by writing a conversation between two very different people saying goodbye to each other (not using speech tags, e.g. he said), then ask someone to tell you what they have been able to learn about them.

Another useful exercise is to write a passage of dialogue giving the same piece of information but from the lips of different characters, e.g. an elderly retired schoolmaster; a precise businessman; a seventeen-year-old girl, and so on.

Emotion

To sell, you only have to...touch the human heart.

Paul Gallico

A piece of fiction that generates no emotion in the reader is one that isn't likely to be successful. It should tug at the heartstrings, cause a shiver to run down the spine, the heart to beat a little faster, a tear to trickle down the cheek. In women's magazine fiction, it is essential and 'strong emotional content' is a phrase that frequently appears in editors' guidelines. But this is not to be confused with sickly sentimentality.

Emotion. The word means 'to move out from'. In the context we are considering, it can be seen as meaning moving our readers out of themselves and into the experiences of another.

'To sell, you only have to...touch the human heart.' There can surely be no better model than Paul Gallico of a successful writer who is able to do just that – touch our hearts. And sell.

The first and obvious point to make is that, if we ourselves don't feel anything for our characters and the situation into which we've put them, it's unlikely the reader will either. In other words, we must care about our characters in order to make our readers care – and care they must if they're going to keep on turning those pages to find out what happens to them.

By the end of this *A to Z* you'll have realised how almost impossible it is to separate the different ingredients that make up a successful piece of fiction. They must blend in the right proportions, as in a cake, if the fiction is to work. Without good characterisation, no one is going to know enough about your main character to bother what happens to him or her. With too little conflict, suspense or tension, or too much description and exposition, the reader will quickly lose interest. In this recipe emotion could, perhaps, be likened to the rising agent without which you'd end up with a flat, lifeless story.

The emotional response engendered in your character (and, as a consequence, in your reader) will stem from the impressions received through the five senses. If your heroine sees the man she loves in the arms of another woman, she experiences heartbreak. If she is alone in a room at dead of night and hears a strange tapping on the window, she is filled with fear. The pungent smell of burning apple-wood swamps your character with nostalgia for her country childhood of twenty years before.

By using the senses appropriately we can develop emotion in our story. By showing our character's *reaction* to that emotion – fleeing from the sight of her lover in another's arms; slamming the bolt on the door and closing the curtains to shut out whatever is trying to get in; letting her dammed-up sorrow for something in the past burst forth into a torrent of tears – your reader will identify with her and experience, vicariously, the same emotion.

When you are writing a scene, you might find it helpful to ask yourself what feelings you want it to eroke. Using a thesaurus to list connected words can be useful because it's easy to run out of synonyms and become repetitive. You need to be subjective, here, because objectivity distances both writer and reader from character and what is happening to him. To ensure this, you will have to enter into your character and their predicament.

The sound came again – tap, tap, tap; like fingernails on the windowpane. But no one could possibly be outside, Selena told herself firmly, as she pulled her shawl closer round her shoulders. No one could reach or climb up to her window. Dan had made sure of that when he'd chopped down the old pear tree that had stood outside for generations. But, if it wasn't a human hand and it wasn't a branch of a tree, what could it possibly be? Selena clenched her teeth to stop them chattering, forcing herself to turn towards the darkened glass. Slowly, she raised her eyes, then froze. In that moment, her heart seemed to stop beating, the blood in her veins to turn to ice and nerveless fingers let the shawl fall to the floor.

I felt more than a twinge of fear, myself, just writing that and wondering exactly what was outside!

The atmosphere you build up in a story also helps heighten the reader's response. Your heroine is tracing her father's footsteps during a fierce guerilla campaign in the mountains of Crete in the last war. Those bare, brooding slopes and rocky peaks will help prepare your reader to respond emotionally to what your heroine subsequently learns took place there. But those mountains, that stony terrain, will also be symbolic of what is happening to her in her own life.

At this point, perhaps we should consider motivation. The word stems from the Latin verb *movere*, to move, as does 'emotion'. Nancy Hale, in *Realities of Fiction*, has this to say:

> If the writer will establish a strong enough motive for action in his...story, he has established a lifeline over which almost anything can be carried. If he fails to establish a strong and acceptable motive, he can save his best writing and his keenest observations; they will not help.

If our character, Selena, is sufficiently afraid, she will *do* something. If she is isn't in the least bothered by strange tappings on the window, she will just sit there and take no action. If your heroine is not deeply in love with the hero, she may feel piqued when she discovers him with another woman but it won't devastate her, causing her to run away, unable to face them.

It is the depth of emotion that provides the motivation for your character's subsequent action. Consider this when you are analysing a story in order to understand why it was published and yours was not. And remember that sentimentality has no depth but is merely a sugary icing on the surface of a story.

Reflect again on Paul Gallico's words; they hold the key to successful fiction-writing: 'To sell, you only have to touch the human heart.'

Top Tip from Catherine Cookson

If you want to touch the heart of a reader, and I think this should be the aim of the writer, then write about the kind of people you know from the inside, whether your acquaintance with them was in the slums, in the middle-class, or in a stately home because then, and only then, will you get your heart into your work. And that is what the reader wants, that is what holds the reader, that is what makes one reader say to another those beautiful words: 'I couldn't put it down.'

Endings

Endings...should concentrate in the reader the impression of the whole.

Anton Chekhov

Chekhov was here talking about the short story where, 99 times out of a 100, it is vital to know your ending before you begin. With the novel, though, whilst most writers have some idea of how it will end, it may well change as the book develops.

What you should aim for is a satisfactory ending: even if it is tragic, it should 'feel' right. If the main character in your short story is a nice guy with a problem, we will all be rooting for him to solve it successfully. If, on the other hand, he's a bad guy, as in the 'biter bit' type of story, we expect him to get his come-uppance and learn his lesson. I once had a student who wrote one about an old lady being conned into selling a valuable antique far below its true worth. Fine – a good beginning and the writer obviously knew his background. However, because he knew it so often happens in real life, he allowed his conman to get away with his fraud and the old lady to be cheated. This student found it hard to understand why the reader would feel let down by such an ending – but let down he would be.

Although the majority of magazine stories have 'happy endings', this isn't strictly necessary provided the main character learns a valuable lesson and it finishes on a note of hope. In a broadcast story of mine, a charwoman desperately longs to own a real fur coat. She finally gets one at a jumble sale and instantly visualises herself as being as grand as the ladies she 'does' for. But a few days later, seeing her coat next to a magnificent fur belonging to a visitor at one of her houses, she realises how moth-eaten and shabby it really is and is heartbroken.

Originally, I sent the story out with this rather downbeat

ending and it was rejected. I put it aside for several weeks, then took it out again, re-examined it and saw that it was too depressing. After all, this valiant little woman had had to struggle to make her dream come true. So, I decided to give it an 'uplift'. I allowed her to accept it was terribly shabby, shed a few tears, then smile again because, as she tells herself at the end, 'It was still musquash, wasn't it?'

Frank O'Connor referred to a story ending as being a 'logical, inescapable flowering of events'. This can be seen admirably demonstrated in one of Somerset Maugham's stories, about a young man who wants to be a great pianist, nothing less will do. When one of the world's leading musicians tells him he will never be more than mediocre, he kills himself. It could have finished with his realising his gift would never take him to the top and accepting it, but that would have been a much weaker ending which would, I suspect, have left the reader dissatisfied.

Finally, if you think through your story first, it's much more likely you'll come up with a more satisfying and logical ending than if you begin without a clear idea of where you are going, especially if it is a short story you are writing.

Flashbacks

The meaning of flashback, according to my dictionary, is: 'a brilliant outburst; to break into one's mind; to light up.' In terms of writing fiction, it means to throw a beam of light backwards into the story that is unfolding. Another definition is: 'a brief interruption in the forward movement of the plot to explain and examine prior events'.

It is a useful and often necessary device for providing information which the reader needs to have in order to understand the motivation behind a character's actions and reactions given that the seeds of contemporary action always lie in past events.

Generally speaking, flashbacks should be used sparingly and kept short, feeding in the information about the past as and when necessary. An experienced writer can sometimes make a complete chapter serve as a flashback, but it needs expertise to carry this off successfully.

With this danger in mind, always introduce some present action that promises future excitement *before* lapsing into the past. And always ask yourself: is a flashback absolutely necessary? If it slows down the action without imparting vital information, then it probably isn't.

Having decided that you need a flashback, set the scene clearly in the past by using the pluperfect (the 'had had') tense to start with:

> It wasn't until that moment that he realised how drastically what had happened on that day, so long ago, had affected her life. He remembered how she had run to him, then, her long golden hair spreading out like gossamer around her face. 'Tom, Tom,' she'd cried, flinging herself into his arms. 'Oh, Tom, I wanted you so much. It's been so terrible...'
>
> He had held her close, comforting her with the warmth of

his body as if to shield from all harm. He had whispered that he loved her, would always love her.

'Oh, Tom,' Marianne sobbed as he kissed her gently...

We are now into the flashback and have changed from the pluperfect to the simple past and can continue in that tense until, towards the end of it, we'll need to signal to the reader that we are about to re-enter the mainstream of the story by slipping back into the pluperfect.

'I don't believe it,' she had whispered...

He'd been cruel, he knew that, but now, looking at a Marianne grown old before her time, he wondered if...

Always try to dramatise a flashback. The 'confession' story is a good illustration of how effective a technique this can be. But take care not to interrupt a dramatic scene that is taking place on-stage to show something that happened in the past. Choose the right moment for it, possibly a moment of introspection on the part of the main character.

Whilst analysing novels for technique and structure, I find it useful to mark in the margin where a flashback starts and ends so that I can see how long it is and judge how effective.

The flashback completed, carry your story forwards by introducing a new piece of action or throw another 'spanner in the works' by introducing some fresh conflict or a new character.

I stress once more, use flashback as a piece of technique applied for a necessary purpose and not because it seems an easy option.

Grammar

A book on creative writing cannot, and should not, be expected to go into grammar in any detail. None the less, there are certain common pitfalls which it seems appropriate to mention. Beyond that there are plenty of good English grammar books and dictionaries on the market, including a new phonetic dictionary for those can't spell sufficiently to find the word they want in a conventional one!

Many people seem uncertain over the correct use of *its* and *it's*. *Whose* and *who's* also give difficulty. In fact, it is simple to distinguish between them as the apostrophe denotes a missing letter – an 'i'. Thus *it's* and *who's* are contractions that we use in everyday speech: *It's* (it is) a good idea to check your spelling. *Who's* (who is) going to teach you to spell?

Its and *whose* are personal pronouns denoting belonging. I hope this book and *its* contents will help you achieve success. *Whose* book will you buy when you are in the bookshop? Simple, really, isn't it?

Accept and *except* are words that are frequently confused. Will you please *accept* my apologies if you know this already but, *except* amongst those who have a degree in English Language, they are often misused.

There and *their* are two more problem words. *There* makes a statement; *their* denotes belonging. *There* are 26 letters in the alphabet. *Their* function is to enable us to create words.

If you know that your grammar and spelling are weak, it is advisable to ask someone more knowledgeable to check your typescript before you send it out. There is no point in prejudicing an editor against your work by submitting it with grammatical errors.

Historical novels

The term 'historical novel' can be said to embrace several forms. It includes historical romances (of the kind published by Mills & Boon under their Masquerade imprint); also novels about people who actually lived and whose exploits, to a greater or lesser degree, are known (Elizabeth Byrd's *The Immortal Queen* or Nigel Tranter's trilogy about Robert The Bruce, for instance). The greatest number, though, will be set in a historically correct background, such as the Civil War or the French Revolution, but peopled with purely imaginary main characters. This latter type gives the writer the most scope for invention. The other sub-genre is what is generally known as the 'period' novel, which is most often set in Victorian or Edwardian times or even later, though prior to the present day.

Clearly, you will choose a period that appeals to you because you will need to do a great deal of research. For some unaccountable reason there seem to be fashions for historical periods though I don't believe one should worry unduly about that. If Jean Auel, when embarking upon her highly successful *Clan of the Cave Bear*, had asked a publisher his opinion as to the chances of a book set in prehistoric times, what would have been his answer? Negative, I suspect. In any case, by the time you've finished writing your book your particular period might be the fashionable one. An acquaintance of mine whose first historical was set in ancient Egypt had to wait twelve years before it was published, presumably because of this fickle business of fashion.

Perhaps the most important aspect to keep in mind is that you must interpret history *from the standpoint of those who lived during it* and not from that of today. Never forget, either, that you are telling a story about people who just happened to live in different times to our own. In other words, the *story* is

67

the thing, however significant the background. Your characters must be as believable as those in a contemporary novel. Their mode of speech, dress, travel, customs and habits will differ, obviously, but emotions and basic drives remain unchanged whatever the age, thus allowing that important common-factor of all fiction – reader-identification – to take place.

Another vital ingredient, as with any work of fiction, is immediacy – the feeling that you are *there*. I remember reading Pat Barr's *Jade* and pulling myself up short to remind myself, incredulously, that she hadn't lived in Tientsin in the 1870s. Yet I felt I was right there with her main character. It gave me an odd sensation and re-emphasised, for me, the wonderful power that some writers have of building illusion, truly eliciting 'willing suspension of disbelief'.

Historical novelists often like to see the places they are writing about. Obviously this isn't always possible but if it is then seize the opportunity. It will help you convey the necessary sense of place. Once when I was researching a period of Scottish history, I went up to the Highlands to walk over the hills and through the glens, through the only bit of the old Caledonian forest extant. I suddenly knew, then, exactly why the Highlanders of old had been such a tough, hardy race, striding across those bare mountainsides, wrapping themselves in their plaids to sleep out there in all weathers, if they had to. And I had the eerie feeling of half-expecting to meet one of them.

The aim of every historical novelist should be to try to create period flavour. To this end, you need to soak yourself in whatever is known about the time and about your characters. Robert Graves admitted that, when he was researching and writing *I, Claudius*, he developed a strange feeling of affinity with Claudius which enabled him to know many things that otherwise he couldn't possibly have known. This indicates how deeply Graves must have immersed himself in the period he was writing about.

An historical novel of any kind is almost certainly 'faction': a blend of fact and fiction. If you've researched thoroughly and found there are certain periods where nothing seems to be known about your main character, there is no reason why you should not make your own deductions as to what might have occurred during those weeks, months or years. Such extrapolations are perfectly legitimate.

One of the main difficulties for an historical novelist is language: how to get the 'feel' of it right, making sure the vocabulary is that which would have been used at the time. A word of modern origin can instantly demolish the illusion of period you've so painstakingly built up, and on the admission of successful historical novelists, it is often easy to let such inaccuracies creep in. In this connection, it is generally agreed that a too-liberal use of 'gadzooks' and 'forsooths' etc. is to be avoided. Your aim must be to give a *flavour* of the speech that would have been used whilst basically writing in standard English. For getting the idiom right, a handy book to consult is the *Dictionary of Historical Slang* by E. Partridge (Routledge). The same author has also written *Slang Today and Yesterday*.

Finally, it boils down to this: are you sufficiently enthralled by history, or one particular era, to undertake the necessary in-depth research? If you are, then it will be a delight and not a chore. It will provide you with hours of fascination as you unearth facts, some perhaps little known, or little stressed, by historians. And there will be all the excitement of the chase as you set off on the trail of yet more background material, some of which may never have been used before.

On of the most comprehensive and convenient libraries for research is The London Library. Its subsciption is fairly expensive but could prove well worth it. Ann Hoffmann's book entitled *Research for Writers*, published by A. & C. Black, is invaluable for telling you where to look for information. There is an excellent series of books on historical dress, customs and so on by Marjorie & Peter Quennell.

Top Tip from Rhona Martin

Author of *Gallows Wedding* (Bodley Head, 1978), winner of the first Georgette Heyer Historical Novel Prize, and of *Writing Historical Fiction* (A. & C. Black).

Historical fiction is perhaps the most demanding, and certainly among the most rewarding, of all the genres. One is faced with all the problems of writing fiction, with a few more added 'just for you'! There is the need to set up an unfamiliar scene without clogging the storyline with unwanted description; there is the difficulty of getting into the minds of people who lived so long ago that even their names sound strange to modern ears; and there is the special question of just how much or how little to concede to archaic language in the dialogue.

The key to solving all these puzzles is to keep in mind that you are writing a story about people, *who were just as human in their time as we are today. Remember that people make history, not the other way about. They and their problems are the paramount concern; anything that gets in the way of reader-identification must be ruthlessly removed, whether it is surplus research (put in because it would be a shame to waste it), an over-reverence for the past which puts the whole scene at a respectful distance, or a too-liberal spattering of 'gadzooks' and 'methinks' and suchlike words which have in themselves become clichés. Get inside your characters and try to feel what they feel, and half your battle is won.*

Horror

Horror stories are basically about the power struggle between good and evil. Are they so perennially popular because they appeal to our worst instincts, allowing us to perpetrate vicariously some of the awful things we occasionally feel we'd like to do? Reader-identification again?

Another reason might be that, right from infancy we like to be frightened, a fact that has been exploited by story-tellers from time immemorial. Doubtless the cave-dwellers embellished their hunting tales as they watched their audience's eyes grow wider and wider. Think back to those well-loved fairytales by the Brothers Grimm and others; how positively gruesome many of them are. *Bluebeard, Hansel and Gretel, Red Riding Hood, Snow White, Sleeping Beauty, Jack the Giantkiller* (to name but a few): all involve wicked witches, monsters, wild animals or cruel people who did, or tried to do, unspeakable things to the innocent. Children's writer, Roald Dahl, has put this knowledge to good use.

While we shiver with fear as we experience at secondhand the terrifying happenings, we are also filled with relief when the protagonist is victorious, when good has triumphed over evil, as happens in all these tales. In the modern adult horror story, however, this is not necessarily so. Occasionally evil wins out and we are left feeling distinctly disturbed by unresolved fears.

Genre fiction of any kind promises certain things: the romance promises a happy ending; the western a climactic fight between the 'goodies' and 'baddies', while the horror story promises a slow, suspenseful build-up to a truly fightening climax. We must not be cheated of this or we will consider the story to have failed.

Tales of the supernatural, which never lose their appeal, can probably be included in this category. They aren't easy to write successfully and the best are probably those which end ambiguously: was it really a ghost or not?

Understatement is usually more effective than painting the scene in all its gory detail. In *The Monkey's Paw*, for instance, that classic tale by W. W. Jacobs, the horror is increased by letting the imagination supply the picture of the awful thing behind the door which is trying to get in.

Stephen King in *Danse Macabre*, his book about the genre, suggests that 'horror fiction is a cold touch with sudden, unexpected pressure'; and, further, that horror is a 'groping for pressure points'. Many of us have the same ones, such as dread of rats or snakes or gigantic spiders, or fear of the dark, which make us feel out of control of our environment. He goes on to say that there is a moral code in the horror tale – that its main purpose is to affirm the virtues of the norm by showing us that awful things happen to those who venture into taboo lands. In other words, there is terrible danger in opening those forbidden doors and the basis of these tales is that there are secrets best left untold.

Study the classic tales of Edgar Allen Poe and Henry James and also those of modern writers such as Roald Dahl, and watch his television series *Tales of the Unexpected*. Peter Straub and Stephen King, of course, are masters of the genre. From time to time, collections of horror tales come out (a recent one entitled *Prime Evil* contains work by these last two writers), and Pan regularly publishes them.

Women's magazines and those aimed at the teenager occasionally seem to like a spine-chilling tale. There is little doubt that, if you can write suspenseful, original tales of horror, you will never be short of a market.

Humour

Of all types of writing, humour is probably the most difficult to bring off and, unless you are a natural humorist, always seeing the funny side of things, success is unlikely. First, of course, there is the problem of subjectivity. What makes one person laugh leaves another cold. So the secret lies partly in finding a subject that has universal appeal. The thoughts and doings of a spotty adolescent suffering the pangs of growing up struck a wry chord of remembrance in many an adult so that *The Secret Diary of Adrian Mole Aged 13¾* quickly became a bestseller.

Humour has its roots in truth and in the seriousness of life. The reader (or listener or viewer) must laugh *with* your characters, not *at* them. They must empathise with their predicament even while shaking their heads at its absurdity.

Humour and pathos should go hand in hand, creating a balance of tensions that make us smile or laugh whilst, at the same time, experiencing a touch of sadness, albeit a fleeting one. Think back to Charlie Chaplin, to Monsieur Hulot, to the highly successful Steptoe and Son sitcom series with the pathetic Harold inextricably caught up in a symbiotic relationship with his dreadful old father and ask yourself if you would have found them and their situations half so funny without the accompanying pathos.

There is no doubt that humorous writing is at a premium, which is why writers of comedy for television are amongst the highest paid, receiving phenomenal fees for half-hour situation comedy episodes. Yet it is just as much a craft that has to be learned as any other genre, even if you are a natural. You have to be able to write about ordinary people in ordinary situations and make them do stupid things. That has to make your reader or audience laugh; sometimes the reaction of others to those stupid things will make the reader or audience laugh even more.

Time and again when judging competitions I've read articles and stories that have tried, and failed, to be funny, mostly because they were laboured. Humour must at least appear to be spontaneous. Generally speaking, it is probably easier to open an article or a script with a punch line and finish it with an even stronger one so that the reader or viewer goes on laughing long afterwards.

Which stories, articles, televised or filmed comic episodes have remained in your memory because they made you laugh long and loud? Try to identify what it was about them that made them so memorable. Once, sitting in an hotel lounge, I laughed out loud when I was reading Lilian Beckwith's *The Sea For Breakfast*. I chuckled for days recalling one particular scene in a Monsieur Hulot film, and the late much-lamented Tommy Cooper could have me rolling off my seat at his inanities. The reason in each case, I think, was that it could have been me in those situations doing the same stupid things. A question once more of reader-identification, together with a feeling of relief that it isn't oneself but another poor soul making a fool of himself?

If you do have a natural talent for making people laugh, you have been blessed with a priceless gift and should nurture it, hone it and, in time, reap the rewards of making it work for you. Editors are like prospectors, longing to find the gold nugget of real humour amongst those heaps of unsolicited typescripts.

Ideas

'Where do you get your ideas from?' That is a question beginner-writers frequently ask and often it's this apparent lack of ideas that seems to prevent them from getting down to writing. This is where belonging to any kind of writing group, be it circle or class, can be invaluable because it is likely that subjects will be set for 'homework'. I know that my own students never let me forget to suggest a theme or set an exercise to help them produce a piece of writing for the following week, saying they wouldn't do anything otherwise. But why should there be this dearth of ideas? I suspect it is partly due to lack of confidence, resulting from our schooldays when we were given specific subjects for 'composition' and didn't have to think them up for ourselves. However being given a set topic always produces a crop of surprisingly diverse results, no two responses being alike in either form or content.

It seems to me that most people, especially beginners, merely need some kind of stimulus to get their imaginations working, so I will now try to suggest a few 'triggers' and, at the end, will give a list of topics that have proved stimulating in my classes.

Short newspaper reports, especially those in the tabloids, can be a rich vein to tap. Scan the pages and cut out any that might provide the germ of a short story. For example: a report about an elderly man barricading himself into his home with his dog which the council say he must get rid of. Another about some villagers who have set up a twenty-four-hour watch to prevent the threatened felling of a 100-year-old chestnut tree which the council insists has grown too large. And one of my favourites (tucked away to use, one day) is about two Santa Clauses having a fight in a crowded high street because of a dispute over a particular pitch. Can't you just see that scene and imagine the reaction of any young children observing it? It simply begs to be written up as a humorous short story.

Another method to get a short story under way is to take the first line of a published one and go on from there: use the idea or the feel of the line, not the line itself, of course. Another is to ask someone to produce three disparate objects and weave those into a story: a wallet, a faded rose, a walking stick, for instance.

To get ideas for 'confession' stories, read the problem pages, those fascinating 'Agony Aunt' columns that many magazines and some newspapers have. They are an excellent source of material for fiction based on real-life problems. They also tell you what subjects the editor is likely to be interested in, the readership to aim at and, therefore, the kind of characters you should write about. For instance, would the editor consider a story dealing with anything as delicate as the colour question or sexual abuse?

Once you start consciously seeking out ideas, you will find them all around you, floating in the ether almost, just waiting for you to reach out and grab them. This is where keeping an Ideas Book becomes invaluable in which you can jot down any snippets of interesting conversation you've overheard in the bus queue, items cut out from a newspaper or magazine, or a few scribbled lines to jog your memory about that marvellous idea you had when you were caught up in a traffic jam or were just going to sleep. If you don't write it down immediately, the chances are it will be erased from your mind forever.

Here is the promised list of subjects, some of which I hope will spark off ideas for articles or for short stories.

If only I'd never...
The Piano
The Move
Stepping Stones
Homesickness
The Anniversary
A day I'll never forget
The Reunion

A Sense of Place

The Visitor

The first time Mr J. saw it, the heath was shrouded in mist. The second time, however, ...

The Door (one that has some special significance for you)

A little bit of luck

A knock on the door or a telephone call that changes your life in a few seconds

The Letter

Roots

The Journey

The Key (one that doesn't fit the lock that it ought to)

The Day the Snow Came

Imagine yourself at a window, looking into a lighted room. Describe the scene and the characters in it and weave a story around them.

Interviewing

Probably the biggest hurdle for the inexperienced is actually asking someone to grant them an interview. The chances are, however, that whoever they approach will be delighted to agree unless they are so famous that they're tired of such requests. That's why, at first, you'd be wise to stick to not-so-well-known people who, nevertheless, have a colourful tale to tell (about an exceptional journey recently taken, perhaps), have an unusual job or perhaps have had a recent success that would be of interest to readers of a magazine or local newspaper.

Keep in mind that, when you invite someone to be interviewed, you are asking them to talk about themselves and their work, travels or achievements, and that few can resist an opportunity like that.

Write or telephone (the former is probably more likely to succeed), politely asking for a short interview and saying for which publication it is intended. Even if at this stage you have not actually got an editor interested, you should have a good idea which one is likely to be. Suggest an hour as being the time you feel you'll require. You'll be able to judge as the interview proceeds whether or not it's going so well that it could continue without causing annoyance.

Once you've arranged a time and place (the interviewee's home is probably best, if possible, because they will be more relaxed, there), start doing your homework so that you don't go in 'cold'. Find out everything about him/her that is already general knowledge so you don't irritate by asking unnecessary questions. You can always ask, briefly, for corroboration of any points about which you don't feel one hundred per cent certain. 'I believe the first time you sang the role of Rodolpho in *La Bohème* was at Sadlers Wells in 1973?' That will also give you a lead into the next question. 'How did that come about?'

Prepare a list of questions in advance and memorise them before you go. Inevitably, they will spark off others you hadn't thought of but at least you won't be caught searching your mind, frantically, for what to ask next.

Ask about their hobbies, how they relax in their leisure time, if they have any pets (animal-lovers will usually talk for hours on that subject, if you'll let them, but you should be able to subtly steer them in the direction you want), and so on.

There are various methods that can be used for interviewing. Some people use a small cassette tape-recorder which they place in an unobtrusive position before the session begins, but *always check first* if this is acceptable because not everyone likes having their words recorded in this way. Most interviewers use a notebook, if only to jot down keywords to which they can refer later. Keywords only is a good idea as the sight of someone scribbling madly can be off-putting. In any case, whilst you are writing you might be missing a significant point. But statistics or technical information *always* need to be written down clearly and legibly to make sure you report them accurately.

As soon as you've left, find a quiet place (a nearby café, perhaps, if you're some distance from your home) and write up your notes in greater detail, especially if you haven't used a tape-recorder. It's all too easy to forget some of the information you've been given if a longish period is allowed to elapse.

The most important thing to remember is the necessity for putting the other person at ease and however nervous you are yourself not to allow it to show. Don't begin by instantly asking questions. Start by introducing your subject obliquely. The first interview I ever did was with a woman who had set up her own animal-rescue centre which she was running on a shoestring. I can't remember exactly how I began but a suitable opening gambit might have been: 'I always resented my parents not letting me have a dog when I was young but I suppose that wasn't necessarily a bad thing. I expect you wish more parents thought like that?' I've no doubt that lady would then have waxed eloquent on the subject and I wouldn't have needed to do more than prompt her, from time to time, to continue.

Finally, as you are leaving, thank them for their co-operation and offer to let them see the finished write-up before you send it off. Not only is that polite but it is also expedient in case you have inadvertently misquoted or got some facts or figures wrong.

Journals

Most of us, at some point, have kept a diary or journal (give it whichever name you like – diary comes from the Latin *dies*, day, while journal is from Old French, derived from the Latin *diurnalis* of similar meaning) in which we recorded our thoughts, feelings and observations. The practice is, perhaps, particularly prevalent at those periods in our lives when we feel the need to make sense of what is happening to and around us and when, for whatever reason, we cannot articulate our resultant anxieties. Such journals, if published, can be fascinating. Take, for example, *Mrs Milburn's Diaries: An Englishwoman's Day-to day Reflections, 1939-45*. Originally intended for her eyes only and therefore written without inhibition, it makes gripping reading.

Many diaries and journals have acquired worldwide fame, such as those of Samuel Pepys, Virgina Woolf, Dorothy Wordsworth, Evelyn Waugh and Anne Frank, not to mention, in another category, Sue Townsend's fictional diary of Adrian Mole.

Keeping a journal is one way of setting down on paper our deepest and most powerful emotions, emotions that will inevitably fade with time but upon which, as writers, we will want to draw later. By also recording details of weather, places, physical descriptions of people we've met, ours and their reactions to events, scraps of overheard dialogue and so on, we are furnishing ourselves with an inexhaustible source of material for our future writing.

Graham Greene in his *In Search of a Character: Two African Journals* (Bodley Head/Penguin Books) shows his thought processes when he was planning a novel set in Africa. In his Introduction, he says: 'I took advantage of the opportunity to talk aloud to myself, to record scraps of imaginary dialogue and incidents, some of which found their way into my novel.' He goes on to admit his regret at not having kept notes during another period of his life in Africa which would have been useful to him when he began to write *The Heart of the Matter*.

Another journal of great interest to any would-be novelist is John Steinbeck's *Journal of a Novel* (Heinemann/Pan Books) which resulted from the warming-up process he devised while he was working on *East of Eden*. It consists of daily letters to his friend and editor, written on the lefthand pages of a notebook which allowed him, when he had flexed his mental muscles, to progress to the text of the novel's first draft on the righthand side.

In my creative writing classes some of the best and most vivid work has resulted from the keeping of a detailed journal for just one day. This was probably because it made everyone conscious of tiny details, small incidents, actions, reactions and impressions that, normally, would have been quickly forgotten yet which added a richness and colour to the tapestry of that particular day.

Anaïs Nin, who kept a journal from the age of eleven until she was seventy-three, believed that a writer is trying to create a world he can live in. She also suggests that, through our writing, we are able to experience life twice as we reproduce the actual moments lived and that, by writing, we heighten our awareness of life.

Keeping a journal is also good therapy, allowing us freedom to let off steam, vent our anger, express our secret loves and hates and fears. But we must be honest. If once we start editing what we write, the diary loses much of its value. Describe what is happening in your life *as it is*, not how you'd like it to be. In modern parlance – tell it how it is.

You might also try writing a fictitious one by the main character in your book, thus providing a means of getting to know him or her as intimately as you know yourself.

Consider this comment at the end of Graham Greene's Introduction to his *African Journals:* 'He [the novelist] goes through life discarding more than he retains, but the points he notes are what he considers of creative interest at the moment of occurrence.' Then use your own journal as a means of talking to yourself in the way that he did.

Finally, remember that keeping a journal can be an excellent means of priming your creative pump, as John Steinbeck discovered when struggling with *East of Eden*.

Kill off your characters

I have acquired a reputation amongst my students for killing off their characters. The reason is a simple. Time and again beginner-writers bring into a story one or more characters who have such minor roles that if they are made to disappear their absence is not noticed. The following fairly typical beginner's scenario illustrates my point.

Heroine's car breaks down as she's on her way to an important engagement. Along comes a helpful passing motorist who is introduced as Ian Johnstone. He tows her to a nearby garage where Dave Smith, the mechanic, tells her what is wrong and how long the repairs will take. Heroine then telephones her sister to explain why she'll be late arriving.

'Jenny, it's me – Sara. Listen. I'm going to be late, I'm afraid. I've broken down at Melchester and...'

'Oh, Sara – that really is too bad,' Jenny broke in waspishly.

It is possible, of course, that Jenny has an important role to play in the plot that is unfolding. If she hasn't, however, then we shouldn't learn what was said between them over the phone. But it is almost certain that Ian Johnstone and Dave Smith will never be mentioned again and therefore should not have come into the story at all.

In a novel, naturally, there is more latitude for introducing one or two very minor characters because they can add verisimilitude to the picture being created. In a short story, though, you cannot allow yourself such freedom. All the characters in a short piece of fiction must pull their weight. If they don't, be ruthless and kill them off. Your story will be greatly improved.

Letter pages

Many magazines have a page reserved exclusively for readers' letters for which payment in some form is offered. Usually there is a larger sum of money or a 'star prize' for the best one published in each issue.

Although this is a relatively small market, none the less it can prove very worthwhile in terms of prizes received, as well as in pleasure at seeing one's efforts in print. Moreover there is a definite skill in writing these short pieces. They have to make their point in a very few words, and be correctly slanted for their market. It takes as much market-study, pruning and polishing to be successful with these as it does with an article.

Sometimes you may want to write about a certain incident which hasn't enough substance for an article, even a short one of around 600 words. Pithily written, however, it may be suitable for a letter-page slot.

A seventy-year-old student of mine was rewarded with an elegant gold wristwatch for one such letter. As it was her first-ever acceptance, the delight and confidence it gave her far outweighed the monetary value of the watch itself.

Don't dismiss these outlets for your writing, especially when you are setting out. Be on the look-out for them wherever you can (doctors' and dentists' waiting rooms are often a good source for unusual magazines). Examine letters published in them carefully to see the readership aimed at, the number of words used and the subjects covered. Rack your brains to come up with a suitably amusing or thought-provoking anecdote, then go home and write it up. It might result in that first magic letter of acceptance.

Literary agents

Opinions differ as to the value of having an agent to handle your work. Some authors consider them to be worth every penny of the 10 per cent commission they usually charge, while others feel they don't do enough to earn it. The real problem lies in finding a reputable one who will take you on if you have no track record in the publishing world. After all, they are in business to make a living and, unless they see you as a potentially successful writer, they will be unlikely to invest time and money in you.

If you have written a novel and feel you would prefer to use an agent rather than try it out with publishers yourself, write to several of those listed in either the *Writers' and Artists' Year Book* or *The Writers' Handbook*, briefly outlining the book. Mention any successes you've already had and ask if they would be interested in handling your novel. If you've had a personal recommendation to a particular agent, which is much the best way of finding one, mention that.

However, don't be surprised if none of them is interested – although once you are a published novelist you'll probably have no difficulty at all in being accepted onto someone's list.

Market study

Writers of articles and stories normally find an outlet first and then write specially for it. This method is not essential provided you make an in-depth study of a particular market *before* you submit your work. It may be accepted, perhaps after a small amount of re-writing to give it an appropriate slant. But, however you go about it, study your market you must if you are to stand more than an outside chance of being successful.

First it is important to identify the readership of potential publications. The advertisements they contain will give a clue to this. Knowing the sex, age and socio-economic group of a magazine's readers enables you to aim your work accurately. For instance, it is pointless sending a story about a teenager and her boyfriend problems to a magazine catering for older women. It is equally useless submitting a thriller or a collection of short stories to a romantic-fiction publishing house, or fiction of any kind to a non-fiction publisher. Yet every week piles of totally unsuitable material land on editors' desks because authors have not done any research. This is not only a stupid waste of time, money and effort, it also demonstrates a lack of professionalism. If you want to enter the market place with your writing, then set about it just as you would if you were going into any other kind of business.

At first be content to aim low and search for unusual and out-of-the-way magazines that aren't found on newsagents' shelves: house magazines, for instance, and trade journals. Local newspapers often take the occasional feature article; be aware of this, not only in your own locality but when you visit another part of the country. Look also for slots in magazines where readers' contributions are encouraged. They may not pay a vast amount but, at this stage, that doesn't matter, does it? The important thing is to get your work accepted.

Finally, here is a checklist of points to help you study your market.

1 Carefully study at least six issues of a magazine before attempting to write for it and take note of the sex, age and socio-economic group at which it is aimed.

2 If it uses both fiction and non-fiction, note the proportions.

3 Note the ages of the main characters and viewpoints used in the fiction.

4 Note the length and type of the stories and articles used.

5 Note the style in which articles are written – 'chatty', informative, erudite.

6 Before submitting a novel, look along the shelves in libraries and bookshops and make sure you send it to a firm who publishes your category of book: thriller, western, contemporary romance, detective, historical novel, or whatever. If it fits their list, it's likely to stand a far better chance of acceptance.

The novel

A good novel tells us the truth about its hero but a bad novel tells us the truth about its author.

G. K. Chesterton

Probably every writer dreams of having his name on a book one day, no matter how many articles and short stories he or she has published, but few start off with a novel and achieve success right away. Most find they need to learn their craft on shorter works and, unless your instincts are sure and your heart is set solely on becoming a novelist, it would probably be wise to follow the more usual path.

However, assuming you are about to attempt a full-length work of fiction, it can be said that, in the case of the 'straight' novel, and leaving aside genre fiction, there are no 'rules'. Here is a vast canvas on which you can splash your wonderful oil-colours as you will (as opposed to the delicate miniaturist technique which is required for the short story) and which lends itself to experimental writing. The latter does not always succeed, of course; possibly much depends on luck or timing (being in the right place with the right book at the right time). But luck and timing are only part of it. Beware of the arrogant certainty which is to some extent in every writer: an unwillingness to accept that maybe their book isn't the masterpiece they think it to be. Sometimes they are right. Kerry Hulme, whose novel *The Bone People* won the 1985 Booker Prize, had that certainty, refused to change any of it, and was eventually proved right. But we should always, I believe, keep that touch of humility that allows us to admit that our lack of success is perhaps because we have not yet fully learned our craft.

Remember that expressing a desire to write a novel is a long way from committing yourself to doing so, spending months and maybe years getting it down onto paper, sacrificing much of your leisure time in the process. So might it first be worth asking yourself – why? Why a novel and not a short story, which would be much quicker to produce? The answer may be that, deep down, you want to write about the truth of your experience, as you see it, and anything shorter than a work of, say, 60,000 words would not give enough scope.

A large proportion of first novels tend to be autobiographical, meaning that they draw upon what the writer has experienced both emotionally and in fact. Using material that is so well-known means you will be closer to the heart of the book, not so likely to make glaring mistakes in background or to invent characters who are not credible. But you will have had a great many vastly different experiences during your lifetime (Pearl Buck once said that no one under the age of forty should attempt to write a book) so how do you choose the one best suited to be the basis of your novel? More than likely, one in particular will have burned itself into your soul and will be clamouring to be exorcised by being written about. But, if you are unsure, you might narrow the field down by considering what has been the most intense experience of your life; one of which you are ashamed, perhaps, or an issue which has remained unresolved. Your story will be a journey to the truth for yourself as well as for your readers.

The chances are that there will be something you are bursting to say, something about life that you have discovered and want to impart to your reader. For example, it might be that you have learned the hard way the wisdom of the Bard's words: 'To thine own self be true'. This is fine so long as you don't end up bible-thumping. *Show* your belief operating in the lives of your characters and your readers will absorb your message unconsciously. Remember Sam Goldwyn's laconic advice? 'If you want to send a message, call Western Union.' Flaubert put it less telegraphically in his *Intimate Notebook* (and what fascinating reading writers' notebooks make): 'If you begin your book telling yourself it must prove this or that…you will write a bad book, because in composing it you have offended against truth, distorted the facts.'

Next we should consider what are the essential differences between a novel and a short story because, when playing around with ideas for fiction, often we aren't sure if they are best suited to book or short story length. Eventually you will develop an instinct for this. Probably the most significant difference lies in the element of time. A novel is able to show characters in a number of crucial moments during their lives whilst the short story should only encompass one. Even in a book which spans but a few hours, such as Nina Bawden's *Afternoon of a Good Woman*, the canvas is broad encompassing, by clever use of flashback, events that have led up to the present situation.

Now let's take a look at some of the aspects of the novel that must be borne in mind whilst writing it.

CHARACTERS

These must be believable and their actions credibly motivated. They should be sufficiently differentiated so that the reader has no difficulty in distinguishing between them.

VIEWPOINT

If you decide on the first person, bear in mind its limitations as well as its advantages – and stick to it throughout. (See Viewpoint, pp. 171-6) When using the third person, avoid jumping around from scene to scene. It is probably best, with a first novel at any rate, to stick to one character's viewpoint throughout an entire chapter. Whenever you do switch, do so for a purpose – because you feel it is through that particular character that you can best bring the scene to life.

Remember that a change in viewpoint temporarily lowers the interest, even if only slightly.

STRUCTURE

This is where many beginners fall down. Despite what I said

earlier about rules, all writing needs a framework, a basic structure, or it will collapse beneath the weight of even the most beautiful words and phrases.

The structure consists of a series of crises, building up to peaks, to small climaxes, then dropping down a little with each minor resolution until the final climax, the highest point in the book is reached, followed by the last resolution, thus bringing the story to a satisfying conclusion.

Outlines

Although no publishers of fiction will accept a book on the strength of an outline and sample chapter(s) unless they are familiar with the author's work, it is quite normal for a non-fiction book to be commissioned in this way. But, even if you have completed a novel, you will still need to send a synopsis or outline either with a query letter (q.v.) or with the entire typescript. In the latter case, it allows an editor to see at a glance if it is likely to be suitable for their list without having to read a large section of the book.

A few publishers, notably those of romantic fiction, are prepared to look at an outline and the first three chapters and, if they like what they see, encourage the writer to send them the completed book. But many writers seem to find great difficulty in working out a synopsis in advance, especially as they suspect they are likely to stick to it as the novel proceeds.

Individual authors and publishers differ as to how much to put into an outline or synopsis. To accompany a query letter about an already completed novel, a couple of paragraphs may suffice. Where only the first three chapters have been written, I would suggest a more detailed synopsis is likely to be more effective in gaining a publisher's interest.

Outlining a story before you begin to write it makes sense. After all, it's unlikely you'd attempt a journey of any length without a map or at least some directions, and a story outline is a comparable guide to prevent you losing your way *en route*.

Phyllis Whitney, in her excellent *Guide to Fiction Writing*, tells how at first her ideas used to fizzle out rather quickly because she didn't know, in advance, where she was going. She admits to having had frightening 'dry spells' when nothing moved (what writer has never experienced the dreaded 'writer's block'?) and needed to find a way to keep her story growing so this wouldn't happen. She goes on to tell how she didn't get to grips with this problem until she began teaching a writing class and needed to be able to help her students find a system for tackling a full-length novel. By encouraging them to plan the structure of their novel throughout the length of an otherwise empty notebook, she found that they were then much better able to develop their stories without losing direction or coming up against frustrating blind alleys.

It is my own belief that most writers benefit from having on paper a detailed outline of their proposed novel before beginning to write it. Some find this method too restrictive, of course, and if they never experience this problem of running dry then they should carry on in their own way. It is for those who, like myself, feel happiest with some sort of plan in front of them that I suggest they try working out the main action and conflicts of their novel, chapter by chapter. Even a couple of sentences for each chapter would enable them to see where they are going, where the high points of the book will come and how the storyline is going to develop.

So far as non-fiction books are concerned, unless you are willing to risk wasting a good deal of your time, it is imperative to get a publisher interested, in the first place, by furnishing him/her with a comprehensive outline of your proposed book, plus some evidence of your capabilities and style, perhaps through some previously published articles on the subject and/or a couple of sample chapters. That way, if he likes your ideas sufficiently, he may well commission the book and add his own suggestions from his greater knowledge of the book trade.

Perseverance

There is a tale of how Dashiell Hammett (author of *The Maltese Falcon*), when he was starting out, received so many rejections that he decided to make a list of all the possible markets for his mysteries, putting the best-paying ones at the top. As each story returned, he sent it straight out again to the next on the list. Once, having worked through the entire list, he began again at the top: this time, the story sold to the first magazine. So, what does this prove? Although he had written what he believed was a good story, it had been rejected many times (possibly owing to the vagaries of the different editors), he had faith in it and in himself and refused to take 'no' for an answer.

Stories abound in the literary world of how books by now-famous authors were turned down again and again until, on the nth time out, they were accepted, eventually becoming bestsellers.

If you had a manuscript returned with 'Strongly advise author not to take up writing as a career' scrawled across the back page in red ink, what would your reaction be, I wonder? Would you accept that piece of cruel, didactic advice and give up? Luckily for us, Catherine Cookson did not when exactly that happened to her with one of her early manuscripts. She cried her eyes out, she says, and stopped writing for a fortnight. Then she said to herself: 'What do they know?' and began again with fierce determination, going on to become one of our best-loved and most successful writers.

On a different scale, when I was writing for a group of similar magazines, often enough a short story would be returned as 'unsuitable for us' and, a week or so later, would be accepted by a sister magazine. However, sometimes it would be rejected by each one in turn, in which case I would file it away for several months. Then I would take it out again re-read it carefully and, after this period of time, objectively. If I believed it was written as well as I could make it, I would re-type, give it a different title and send it off again. Frequently, it was accepted on this second time around. Again, one has to acknowledge that an editor's judgement is, to some extent, subjective.

A friend of mine who wrote feature articles for newspapers and magazines in her 'spare' time (she was also a doctor's wife with a family) wrote a piece on a subject she felt strongly about. It was rejected nineteen times. On the twentieth, it was accepted by a top national newspaper. She has a maxim worth repeating: 'Keep sending it out because it won't sell sitting in a drawer!'

BUT (there's always a 'but', isn't there?) there is a corollary to that. You must learn to be your own best critic and to be honest with yourself. As a writer, there is a fine line to tread. On one side of it lies your faith in what you have written while, on the other, there is the acceptance of the possibility that maybe it isn't quite good enough, needs to be worked on some more or put away for a while until you've learned a little more about your craft.

In the end, it is up to you to decide but of one thing I remain unswerving in my conviction: if what you have written is good enough, it will sell somewhere, at some time. To make that happen, all you need is perseverance.

Top Tip from Margaret Thomson Davis

Author of *The Making of a Novelist* (Allison & Busby, 1981).

I'm always astonished at people who tell me that they have tried to be a writer and failed because they had their book rejected by a publisher. One publisher! I assure them that it is when their book has been rejected by a hundred and one publishers *that they should begin to worry. Although, of course, I know only too well the disappointment, the discouragement and the abject sense of failure that beginner writers feel. I've experienced all those things myself. Rejection can be a terrible blow to the self-confidence. But, if you want to be a published writer, you have to realise that the first essential is perseverance.*

Believe it or not, a one point in my writing life, I had ten *novels bouncing back and forth between London and Glasgow. It was during that time that I shed some broken-hearted tears and said to myself, 'You're a fool. You have no talent. You'll never be a writer!' Yet, at the same time, steel entered my soul and I began repeating to myself, 'Yes, I will! I will! I will!' This is the kind of determination I believe you need to succeed.*

Plagiarism

To plagiarise, according to my dictionary, is to appropriate and give out as one's own the writings of another. Plagiarism is literary theft and is the worst thing any writer can be accused of. Certainly the only time I have ever wept at a criticism of my work was when that charge was levelled at me. It is possible that one can in all innocence use someone else's plot, which has lain in the subconscious for years after reading the original, probably because you found it so impressive. This is a genuine fear of many writers. I well remember my own horror at wondering if I had done just that: I got into my car and drove twelve miles to my nearest reference library to find a copy of the play I was supposed to have plagiarised. I remember, too, the enormous relief at finding that my play bore little resemblance to the other except that both involved a woman shoplifting.

It is not plagiarism to use a basic plot (after all, according to Georges Polti, there are only thirty-six, anyway) and weave your own story around it, with different characters, backgrounds and situations. Romantic novels, for instance, make constant use of the Cinderella story, of the 'arranged marriage', and so on, and their authors can hardly be accused of stealing. But to take a published story, 'lift' it virtually in its entirety and then send it to an unsuspecting editor merely proves someone is a good cheat, not a good writer.

I'm sure this doesn't happen often but, from time to time, it does and in so flagrant a form that one can only wonder at the perpetrator's audacity. However, no one with a genuine desire to become a writer would stoop to such depths and I have only mentioned the subject out of general interest and as a warning to watch that your subconscious doesn't catch you out.

Plotting

A plot is merely the manipulation of our raw materials in order to achieve the maximum response from the reader.

Walter Pitkin

E. M. Forster in *Aspects of the Novel* wrote 'A plot is a...narrative of events, the emphasis falling on causability.' Elizabeth Bowen suggests that 'Plot is the knowledge of destination.'

Many writers start their novel with only the vaguest idea of where it will lead, much of the excitement for them lying in discovering their destination as they write, whilst others make a detailed outline, mapping the book out chapter by chapter. Most probably fall somewhere between the two, like Rosemary Sutcliffe who has said that, before she starts, she has a basic framework, knows her ending and one or two ports of call on the way.

Note the word 'causability' used by E. M. Forster; it is a keyword in plotting. What will get the book off the ground, set its wheels in motion, is an event outside the main character's jurisdiction, beyond his power to control, which then triggers off a series of *causally-linked* happenings. This has the effect of a pile of dominoes collapsing once one has been removed.

How to set about plotting is up to the individual but I suspect that, for a first novel, most will find it easier to plan in fairly great detail, even if the plan is only loosely followed once writing is in progress. Maybe it's a matter of personality, but I know that I feel more comfortable doing it that way. Phyllis Whitney, in her helpful *Guide to Fiction Writing*, suggests keeping a planning notebook. Hers contains sections on plotting, characters and a detailed outline of the book in which she scribbles down any odd ideas that occur to her which she thinks she might be able to use at some point in the story. She has other sections, too, but she considers these three to be the heart of her notebook system and says they prove invaluable whenever she meets a 'dry spell'. Indeed she devised this system to help her through those difficult and not-uncommon patches of 'writer's block', which can be extremely frightening and even, on occasions, lead to the abandoning of a novel. I have adopted this method myself and found it very effective. I have since learned of others also using it as a means of maintaining fluency and of pre-planning incidents they think they may use at a later stage in their book.

In a similar way Paddy Kitchen, author of *The Way To Write Novels*, writes paragraphs and short pieces which she then puts away in a folder. She has no idea where in her book they will fit but knows, instinctively, that they will be used at some point.

Each of us must devise our own way, but at least we can look at how others work and adapt their methods to suit ourselves, if we feel it will be helpful.

FIRST DRAFT

Someone has said that first drafts only exist to be rewritten. Most novelists would probably agree with this. But we are all individuals and in this, as in other respects, each has his own particular way of working. Some cannot move on to the next page or even paragraph until the current one is as perfect as they can make it. Most, I suspect, rush through their first draft in order to get the story down on paper whilst it is white-hot and only then go back to revise and restructure.

I have heard of someone who writes his first draft on the lefthand side of a notebook, adding notes or 'brushstrokes' as he goes along on the righthand side, but otherwise leaving it blank for when he comes to expand. This, it seems to me, is an excellent method if one writes in longhand, and easily adapted if one types or uses a word processor.

Clearly, all aspects of the craft of novel-writing, as with other types of fiction, necessarily overlap. Although they can be considered individually when analysing and understanding what goes into making a novel, when it comes to the actual creating of your story the elements will be harder to distinguish. It is during the learning process that it helps to take things apart.

Somerset Maugham suggested that the best way to learn about novel-writing was to study the craftsmanship of successful novelists. It should follow, therefore, that the more you read, the more you take things apart, the more likely it is that your learning process will bear fruit!

Poetry

A subject as vast and complex as poetry requires an entire book to itself, and one written by a practising and experienced poet. Therefore I have contented myself with a few comments. It is up to the individual reader to take it from there, if he so wishes.

To start with, we might ask if it is possible to define poetry. Many have tried, with only partial success. William Wordsworth put it thus: 'Poetry is the spontaneous overflow of powerful feelings: it takes its origin from emotion recollected in tranquillity.' Thomas Gray maintained that 'genuine poetry is conceived and composed in the soul.'

My dictionary offers a more prosaic definition: 'an imaginative, impassioned and rhythmical expression whether in verse or prose.' In whatever terms you view it, every true poet agrees there is no more difficult or exacting form of writing. Yet many beginner-writers avow that they 'find it easy'. On hearing some of their work read out, it becomes obvious they have spent more time on ensuring that it rhymes than on expressing some meaning or emotion in the best words and form possible. They have written verse or doggerel, not poetry. This is not to say that the former does not have its legitimate place in the sphere of writing. Indeed it does, and often gives much pleasure to both writer and audience – but it cannot properly be graced with the name of poetry.

The frequent obsession with rhyming may stem from a confusion between the functions of rhyme and rhythm. That poetry must have rhythm is indisputable but rhyme it need not. The need for the former becomes clear when we trace poetry's origins. Lyric poetry was originally sung as entertainment at festivities, accompanied by the lyre. Our word 'verse' comes from the Latin 'vers', meaning a furrow. Verse was once a practical method of helping men with their ploughing, much as the negro slaves sang spirituals to ease their labours.

Dylan Thomas said of poetry that it 'helps to extend everyone's knowledge of himself and the world around him.' A good poem shares with us an experience and the writer's emotional reaction to it. But it is a *fresh* reaction. Though the experience may be a common, age-old one the new angle of perception jerks the reader into sharper awareness. The use of language and form to express this reaction is a skilled business requiring much work. In other words, a would-be poet needs to learn his craft.

Regarding craft, Kathleen Raine, one of our most eminent modern poets, has this to say: 'Uncontrolled poetry has no character and carefully worked-on poetry seems spontaneous and has style.'

To recap, then, a poem is the communication of an experience and the feelings engendered by it. It has a musical quality that is not necessarily dependent upon artifically-engineered end-of-line rhyming. It uses fresh metaphors and vivid imagery. It is about the concrete and specific rather than the abstract – about the particular, not the general.

And, lastly, what outlets are there for it? Sadly, very few. However, many magazines print the occasional poem if its theme is suitable. There are numerous competitions held around the country. There are poetry and literary magazines such as *Outposts, Envoi, Stand, Ambit, Prospice* and *Poetry Review* (the Poetry Society's own magazine), although they all receive far more than they can publish.

Whilst no one makes a fortune out of writing poetry, it is probably the best apprenticeship anyone can have for learning to write good prose. However, most poets write it because they must and any money they might receive is considered merely as a bonus.

Presentation

When you send off your work to be considered for publication, it makes obvious sense to take as much care over its presentation as you did over its creation. A well-presented typescript always stands a better chance of being read – or, at least, looked at. Follow these few simple rules:

1   Use the best-quality paper you can afford – bond for preference and definitely not flimsy. Photocopying paper usually makes an acceptable cheaper alternative.

2   The size should be A4 and you should type on one side only. (Submissions should never be handwritten.)

3   Type in double-spacing, not single or one and a half. If your typewriter has three settings, almost certainly you will need no. 3.

4   Don't use a ribbon so worn that the type will give an editor eye-strain: psychologically that gives your typescript an immediate minus. Worn ribbons on dot-matrix printers produce an even more off-putting result.

5   Leave good margins of approximately $1^1/2$ inches (4 cm) on the lefthand side and at least 1 inch ($2^1/2$ cm) on the right and at top and bottom of each page.

6   Number the pages consecutively. That means, in the case of a novel, you should *not* start numbering each chapter afresh.

7   Type the name of the piece at the top of each page. Then if any page comes adrift, it is immediately apparent which typescript it belongs to.

8   Use a cover-sheet for each submission, on which is stated the title, the number of words, your name and address, pseudonym if one is used, the date, and (in the case of a short story or article) the rights you are offering. With a novel there is no need to mention rights at all – the publisher takes it for granted that you are retaining your copyright.

9   Enclose a covering letter, as well as the cover-sheet, with every submission, however short or self-explanatory the piece might be. The letter should explain who you are, what it is you are offering, and why you are offering it; a touch of straight salesmanship might help, but be truthful, and don't exaggerate.

10   Remember *always* to keep a copy for yourself in case your typescript goes astray.

11   Don't staple or rigidly bind the typescript of a novel. Publishers are unanimous in preferring the pages to be loosely held together by a rubber-band and/or placed in a box which has previously held your typing paper.

12   Don't forget to enclose a stamped addressed envelope with a short typescript or stamps to cover return postage of a novel.

13   Finally, when you have assembled everything and are ready to send it all off, just go through it all again, page by page, looking for anything you may have missed first time round. Check for spelling, grammar, continuity, style, look for those things that might annoy you in somebody else's writing: too many exclamation marks, perhaps, too many Is, repeated adjectives, adverbs, clichés. If you see a page you don't like – do it again. A final check might delay you by a day or more, but it could make all the difference between acceptance and rejection. It also gives you that one last chance to be *honest* with yourself, and to ask 'Is it *really* good enough?' Once you're satisfied that

it's the best you can do, then off it goes. Consider the example of the novelist R. K. Narayan, who reads his finished typescript on trains, pretending he is reading something by someone else to see if it is good enough for publication.

Query letter

Many publishers prefer to receive a query letter, in the first instance, rather than a full-length unsolicited typescript. This makes sense all round. It is easier and less time-consuming for them to reply to a letter and it is considerably less expensive for the author, costing only a few pence instead of several pounds for the two-way postage of a book. It also means you can approach any number of publishers, simultaneously, thus saving much time. (Although multiple-submission of completed novels is nowadays more common, this doesn't decrease the expense of postage and of producing extra copies.)

If you receive a favourable reply from one publisher or more, that is the moment to send out the typescript, with the added advantage that a particular editor will be expecting its arrival. This means it won't go onto what is known in the trade as the 'slush-pile' from whence it may receive only a cursory glance from a fairly junior member of the staff.

Keep your letter short and to the point, outlining the plot of your book in a couple of paragraphs at most. If it is written for a specific category (e.g. detective, romance, western), mention this. If you have had works of fiction published, previously, (perhaps a number of short stories in magazines) then say so: it indicates your professional status. Finish by asking if they would be interested in seeing your book. Naturally, you will have done your homework first to ensure that you only write to firms who publish the kind of book you have written.

EXAMPLE QUERY LETTER

Dear

I have just completed a 70,000-word novel entitled '.......'

It is about a family in a Devonshire farming community. The main character is Leo, and the story, which opens in

1920 when he is eight, spans his lifetime of nearly eighty years, during which period he loses, but later regains, the farm which has been in his family for generations.

The story deals with the vicissitudes of farming-life in that period, with Leo's passionate love for a sophisticated city-girl, who loathes the dirt, grinding hard work and lack of any modern conveniences, and with his marriage to another girl more suited to this kind of life.

If you feel this might be suitable for your list, I should be pleased to submit the typescript for your consideration. A similar letter has been addressed to other publishers.

Yours sincerely,

It is important to be honest about having written to other publishers. If an editor is interested, the knowledge of possible rivals may well elicit a quick response.

Always address your letter to an individual by name, if possible. To find out the name of an editor, either telephone the publishing house and enquire, or look in *The Writers' Handbook*.

Radio writing

'The almost telepathic transference of images from mind to mind is the beauty and the glory of the radio play.'

Martin Esslin, The National Theatre of the Air, 1964.

The most vital concept to be grasped in writing for radio is that the words are intended to be heard – not read. It might seem absurd to make such an obvious statement but, none the less, the point is sometimes lost sight of and so needs emphasising. It is always important to be conscious of the rhythm of a piece of writing, be it poetry or prose, but even more so when it is intended for the ear and not the eye. The way the words *sound* is vital: for instance, sibilants coming together are difficult for an actor to enunciate. Take the following as an exaggerated example: 'Sylvia slid down the slippery slope with ease.' On the page, that might look like a deliberate attempt at alliteration but, on the air, it would sound absurd.

I would urge you to read aloud and tape-record whatever you have written for radio. Playing it back will help you listen to it critically.

Work intended for radio should be thought of in terms of time rather than number of words or pages. The programme *Morning Story*, for instance, lasts for fifteen minutes. (Here, however, 2,250 words is roughly the length required for that time-span, with a maximum of 2,500, allowing for possible cutting.)

Radio is both intimate and immediate. The radio audience should be visualised as one person in a room alone, despite the fact that there will probably be thousands of listeners. With no visual aids at all, the writer must create the right atmosphere in the first few moments to capture that person's interest and attention. Unlike in the theatre, there is no audience reaction except the invisible one pithily known in radio and television circles as 'the Oh hell! switch', which says it all. If your listener or viewer isn't 'hooked' within the first two or three minutes, he switches off – or over to another station!

Let's now consider the different forms of radio writing, starting with *Morning Story*. As with any other market, the best advice is to listen to a good many of them to get a 'feel' for what is required. If 10.30 am is not a convenient time for you to listen, ask someone to record some programmes for you.

This is about the only outlet for what might loosely be termed the 'general short story' and it does take a wide range of non-category fiction. As you will realise if you listen regularly, the stories are quite dissimilar in terms of plot and background: no doubt their popularity is partly due to this. A few years ago the BBC attempted to remove *Morning Story* but the public outcry was so great that it was swiftly restored. Because this slot exists, and devours a vast quantity of material each year, it rather makes nonsense of the oft-heard lament that there are no markets for the short story apart from women's magazines. (Perhaps, though, this complaint is a handy excuse for lack of success in the genre.)

But let's take a more detailed look at what is required of a story for radio.

1   Originality of plot – that really goes without saying. There is virtually no situation you cannot use. One writer I know wrote an excellent story about a tramp who wanted to be embalmed instead of buried: a ghoulish-sounding subject but, of course, everything depends on the treatment. I've heard powerful stories on such terrible subjects as child murder, suicide and the problems in Ireland, all handled in such a way that, first and foremost, they made compelling and thought-provoking listening. There is a place for humour, too, to balance the more 'meaty' stories, but remember that humour should be rooted in truth and is not easy to write.

2   An awareness that, if a vital piece of information is missed,

the listener can't turn back to catch it. Therefore, anything of importance should be repeated: the 'tell 'em you're going to tell them, tell 'em and tell 'em you've told 'em' precept. This means you should ease into a radio story rather than plunge in as you might with one for a magazine. This doesn't mean having a long preamble, however, because it is still necessary to catch your listener's attention immediately. Study the way successful stories manage this.

3   Because of the intimacy of the medium, the first person viewpoint is very effective.

4   This intimate nature should be reflected in the language you employ, so it will help to think of yourself sitting at the fireside, relating a tale to a friend.

5   Remember that structure is just as important for a radio story as for any other kind. The storyline needs to be simple but suspenseful, holding the listener in its grip until the end. The greatest compliment I have ever received was learning of someone unknown to me missing her bus because she simply had to stay to find out how my story ended. (Structure is dealt with in detail under the Short Story section, pp. 135-45.)

6   You will not be allowed to read your own story over the air – a professional actor always does this.

Next, we'll turn to drama. Radio is the biggest single market for plays that exists and many well-known TV dramatists got their start there. Again, there is absolutely no situation that cannot be turned into a play for radio because no stage props are needed and the only scene-setting is that which takes place in the mind.

As with the story, originality is at a premium since producers are tired of receiving plays dealing with worn-out themes and plots. When the BBC ran a competition to celebrate fifty years of radio, I remember reading a bitter complaint by Brian Miller, then drama producer at Bristol, that over half the plays entered opened in a domestic setting with the characters seated around a table. So, taking originality as a *sine qua non*, what are the basic ingredients that go to make up the radio play? There are four:

1 Dialogue
2 Silence
3 Sound effects
4 Music

Obviously, by far the most important is dialogue, which will carry the weight of the play, but silence can be very effective in heightening tension and inferring unspoken words. Sound effects (FX) and carefully-chosen accompanying music are useful tools for scene-setting but they should also add something to the script, helping create the right atmosphere. Indeed, every scene, and especially at the beginning, should have at least one ambient sound to create mood and an image of the surroundings and to establish a sense of place. The tune of 'Oh, I do like to be beside the seaside' played on a Compton organ reminiscent of the 1940s and 1950s, for instance, might conjure up a picture of a seaside town or holiday camp filled with rather jolly elderly characters enjoying themselves. Add the sound of a seagull, fairground rides or lapping waves and we learn a bit more. A foghorn, an owl hooting, or churchbells and three totally different pictures are created in the mind.

Whilst the dialogue should appear natural, it must actually contain far more information than it would in normal speech. It should never be put in without a specific purpose, that is, to characterise, provide necessary information or move the storyline forwards.

THEME

Think about what you are trying to say in your play. If it isn't making some oblique statement, it isn't likely to be a good play. Firstly, though, remember that the word 'drama' comes from the Greek 'to do'. Therefore, it is axiomatic that a play will be about people *doing* things: it won't be all talk and philosophising. If your play is about love, make sure it is about a great love; if about hate, about a deep hate; if about ambition, a ruthless ambition. Keep in mind that word of paramount importance – CONFLICT.

CONSTRUCTION

As with any other type of writing, it is important to understand the need to structure a radio play correctly.

When you are about to end one sequence or scene, you need to give your listeners a hint that the action is about to move elsewhere. Then, when it has done so, confirm it (the old: 'tell them...again'). Sound is a useful device to signpost change of scene.

It is important to introduce variety into the script which can be achieved in a number of ways:

–by varying the number and type of characters in a particular scene;
– by having scenes of differing length;
– by setting them in different locations;
– by altering the pace of the dialogue from scene to scene.

To get your play started and the action under way, you need to introduce someone or some event that causes a change in an existing situation, setting off a chain reaction, rather like tossing a stone into a lake which causes ripples to spread out from it. One way is to open with a conversation that builds up to the entrance of a major character. In *The Gingerbread House*, a Giles Cooper Award-winning play by Ken Whitmore, the father is talking to his two children who are supposed to be getting ready for bed. There is a ring on the doorbell and when he opens the door, there stands a woman, the pivotal character around whom the play revolves.

Remember that:

1   If you start low-key, you will have plenty of scope for building up the events in intensity until the climax or highest

point in the play is reached – sometimes referred to as the 'obligatory scene'.

2   By foreshadowing conflict you will increase the tension.

3   You should make sure your characters are as individual as possible, bearing in mind your audience cannot see their physical attributes.

Advice generally given by playwrights is that it is wise to allow your ideas sufficient time to germinate and your characters to develop before you rush to the typewriter. There is a delightful anecdote of how J. M. Barrie was once stopped in the street by someone and asked how his latest play was coming along. 'Oh, I've just finished it,' Barrie replied, blithely. 'I've only got to write it, now.'

Radio is magic. It is like practising sleight of hand only using words instead of props to summon up images out of the ether. It has been said that the best radio writing is by people with poetic vision – but there is room for all kinds of writing on the air.

That radio drama can produce a profound reaction was proved in the 1930s when Orson Welles's dramatisation of *The War of the Worlds* made listeners believe they really were being invaded by aliens from out of space and plunged the whole of America into panic.

Remember that you are orchestrating voices, silences, music and sounds to create the images you want. Avoid using a narrator unless you feel it is essential.

TIMING

Either with or without a tape-recorder, read your script aloud, allowing for sound-effects, for music and silences or pauses, acting out 'business' such as someone walking down a street or shutting a door. Use a clock or stop-watch to make sure your timing is as accurate as possible. It's safer to run over rather than under as you will probably find that, in any case, cutting a scene or a few lines of dialogue will tighten and improve the play. 150 words per minute is an approximate gauge.

MARKETS

There are usually several slots for drama, varying in length from 30 minutes to 90 minutes or even longer. However, perhaps the best outlet for a new writer is provided by *Afternoon Theatre* (45 to 55 minutes) which broadcasts two plays each week, or *Thirty Minute Theatre*, though the latter's structure is as tight as that of the short story. The BBC receives an average of 200 scripts a week, so a waiting period of several months is likely. However, the serious aspiring radio dramatist won't sit around waiting for news of his brainchild but will be engaged upon the next, ready to submit it whether a rejection or an acceptance is ultimately received.

PRESENTATION

1   The script should be typed on A4 paper and on one side only.

2   The names of the characters should be typed in full each time they are used.

3   Include with your play a synopsis and a cast-list with any brief notes on individual characters which you feel are important enough to be mentioned.

4   Long speeches (8 lines and upwards) should be typed in double-spacing; short speeches in single. (In rehearsal scripts, each speech is numbered consecutively, starting afresh on each page, but this is not necessary on a script initially being submitted for consideration.)

5   Submit your script to any of the regions (see *Writers' &*

Artists' Year Book or *The Writers' Handbook*), or to The Script Editor, Radio Drama, Broadcasting House, London W1A 1AA (with SAE, naturally).

EXAMPLE OF LAYOUT OF SCRIPT

INTERIOR. CAR. RADIO PLAYING.
THROB OF ENGINE. TRAFFIC NOISES
OVER MUSIC

1	DEBBIE:	Where's the sea, mummy? Are we there yet? I'm hot. Can I have a drink?
2	ALAN:	Keep her quiet, for God's sake, will you, Clare? This traffic's bad enough without her whining in my ears all the time.
3	F/X: SOUND OF DEBBIE STARTING TO CRY	
4	CLARE:	Hush, Debbie. It won't be long now. Be a good girl for daddy.
5	ALAN:	I knew we should've got away earlier. If we'd got up at five like I said...
6	CLARE:	I'm sorry, dear. But I thought we'd decided not to...
7	ALAN:	Bit late being sorry now.
8	F/X: SILENCE. THEN SQUEAL OF BRAKES. SOUND OF HORN	
9	ALAN:	Hell, what's that damned idiot trying to do?

TALKS

Unfortunately, many of the old slots for 'personal experience' talks, such as *Woman's Hour*, seem to have disappeared. However, if you are an authority on a subject which you feel would make an interesting radio talk, write to the Talks and Documentaries Department at Broadcasting House, enclosing either an outline or the finished script and stating why you consider yourself qualified to give it. If they are interested, you will be given a voice test because you will be required to read your script over the air (pre-recorded, of course).

A talk is basically the same as an article: you need an arresting opening, you should make your theme clear right away, use a conversational style, and evocative language.

All the foregoing applies to the BBC's national network only. Local radio's requirements are obviously different and will vary from station to station. Their fees are usually extremely low, in some cases non-existent, but you would be gaining experience in writing for radio and in the process see a little of what goes on behind the scenes in broadcasting.

USEFUL PUBLICATIONS

The Art of Radio by Donald McWhinnie (Faber & Faber)
Writing for the BBC (BBC Publications, see below for address)
Giles Cooper Award-winning Plays (Methuen in association with the BBC)
Out of the Air – a collection of plays (Longman)
BBC Radio Play Scripts – working scripts, available from BBC Publications, Woodlands, 80 Wood Lane, London W12 0TT.
Notes on Radio Drama, available from The Script Editor, Radio Drama, Broadcasting House, London W1A 1AA (enclose SAE).

Notes on *Morning Story* are available from the Producer, *Morning Story* at the same address.

Revision

Often must you turn your stylus to erase if you hope to write something worth a second reading.

Horace

Writers differ in their methods of working. Some revise as they go along, unable to proceed further until each sentence, each paragraph and page are as polished as they can make them. Most, however, get their story down on paper in its first draft form, not worrying too much about grammar or spelling, leaving spaces where the required word doesn't spring to mind instantly. When they have completed this more creative part of their work, then they begin the task of revising and re-writing. This involves pruning and polishing, cutting out adjectives, substituting strong verbs for adverbs, ruthlessly eliminating or expanding scenes as necessary, 'killing off' characters who have no real part to play in the story and checking for grammatical mistakes and poor syntax.

Hemingway likened writing to sculpting: you mould the material into your basic shape, first, and then re-work and refine it. He, like many others, always went over what he had written the previous day before carrying on from where he had left off. And he had a little trick, which is worth considering. He always finished each day's work while the creative juices were still flowing freely, leaving it in the middle of a sentence or paragraph so that, the following morning, he could quickly pick up the thread.

In *Writers at Work: The Paris Review Interviews,* Hemingway admitted that he had re-written the last page of *A Farewell to Arms* thirty-nine times before he was satisfied with it. Asked what it was that had stumped him, he replied: 'Getting the words right!'

Interviewed for the same series, Georges Simenon remarked that his main job when he re-wrote was to cut out 'adjectives, adverbs and every word which is there just to make an effect... You have a beautiful sentence – cut it,' he said.

'The purpose of first drafts is to be rewritten.' Remember this and you'll be in the company of by far the vast majority of successful authors, though there does come a time when you have to say to yourself: 'That's it. I can't tinker with it any more, or it'll never be finished.' You've written and re-written it, put it away for a few days (or, preferably, a few weeks) in order to help you look at it more objectively and critically, revised it until it is as perfect as you honestly believe you can make it and now it's time to put it to the ultimate test – send it out and get on with the next piece.

Here are ten points to help you with revision:

1   Cut out adjectives and adverbs where they don't add vital colour and tone to your writing.

2   Check for spelling and grammatical mistakes. If necessary, ask someone knowledgeable to go over it for you.

3   Cut out superfluous dialogue in your fiction.

4   Re-word or re-structure awkward-sounding phrases or sentences.

5   Check for repetitions. In an article, especially, they can become extremely tedious and it's usually possible either to find alternative expressions or to omit them where the meaning is clear.

6   Avoid so-called 'purple passages', those self-indulgent bits of 'fine writing' we all fall in love with from time to time. In the words of Quiller-Couch: 'Murder the darlings'.

7   Remove anything that smacks of preaching or 'tub-thumping'. No one is likely to be interested in your opinions unless they have been specifically asked for.

119

8   Cut out any information that isn't relevant to the plot of your story. This is likely to be a pitfall when you have done a lot of research and don't want to waste any of it.

9   Get rid of any characters who aren't essential to your story's development.

10   Put your piece of work away for a while to enable you to take a fresh and objective look at it before you put it in an envelope and send it off to an editor or publisher. If you feel another re-write would improve it, grit your teeth and do just one more. That little bit of extra work might make the difference between acceptance and rejection.

Romantic fiction

'Love makes the world go round' is an old saying and, despite the soaring divorce rate, romance appears to be as much in fashion as it ever was. Indeed, the more difficult life becomes, the more we all need some form of escapism. Romantic fiction provides just that for many women, as does James Bond and fiction of that ilk for men.

There is a belief among the uninformed that it is easy to write and that 'anyone can do it'. Well, the proof of the pudding is in the eating, as they say, so if you are one of those who think it is simple, put it to the test and try! If you find yourself in difficulties perhaps you will turn back to this page and read on.

First of all, let's not pretend that there isn't a great deal of money to be made if you 'hit the jackpot' and have your work accepted by the crème de la crème, Mills & Boon, because there is. (Remember, though, there are many other publishers of romantic novels, both here and in the USA, at whom you can aim, all of them looking for high-quality writing, believable heroes and heroines and the obligatory 'happy endings'.) But apart from money, what other advantages are there in writing romances? One is that, having learned your craft with this genre, there is nothing to prevent you from going on to try a 'straight', historical or other kind of novel, as many others have done.

Turning to our study of the form, we will look at the contemporary category romance of between 30,000 and 50/60,000 words.

VIEWPOINT

A romantic novel centres around the hero and heroine but, essentially, it is her story and is told from her viewpoint; that is, through her eyes. Occasionally, an experienced writer will slip briefly into the hero's viewpoint but this is not the norm and it might be wiser, at this stage, to avoid doing so. Most romantic novels are told in the third person although one or two imprints (*Woman's Weekly* Library Series, for example) publish stories written in the first person. The reason for the third person being the most popular is that it more readily allows the reader to identify with the heroine and to make-believe that this wonderful hero could also be hers. However, as always, you should keep up with market requirements. If you are unsure about the whole concept of viewpoint, it is dealt with more fully under that heading (see pp. 171-6).

HEROINE

As she is your most important character, you need to know her as well as you know yourself. Finding the right name for her is essential and many writers say that the book won't work until they do. Frequently they are rather fanciful names or at least have been shortened to an unusual sobriquet. Take a quick look at some used in recent novels. Samma (short for Samantha); Christabel; Freddie (short for Frederica); Laurel, Catriona. When you have a clear picture of her in your mind, try to find the name that suits her best. Cristabel, for instance, conjures up for me a tall slender redhead, while Freddie might be a vivacious leggy blond. Names, as we've already discussed, carry certain connotations in the minds of most people so the wrong one could destroy the image you are striving to build.

As well as her name and physical appearance, what are her emotional and psychological attributes? Is she quiet and slow to anger or volatile in temperament? Is she fond of all animals but especially cats? What are her secret fears, her likes and dislikes, rational or otherwise? Has she any family and, if so, does she live with them or in a flat or bedsit of her own? Build up a mini-biography of her in some detail. The Mills & Boon guidelines (available on cassette) suggest you should even know her size of shoe.

In today's stories, it is not necessary for her to be a virgin (unless you want her to be) but she must not have slept around.

She may have been involved, previously, in a serious relationship which has foundered. She may be engaged but for some reason, whilst believing herself to be in love with fiancé, be holding back from the ultimate sexual commitment. She may even be widowed and have had an unsatisfactory marriage. She must, however, be spunky, with plenty of initiative and not sitting around waiting for a prince on a white charger to ride up and rescue her or sweep her into marriage.

Just as in any kind of novel, your main character (in this case, your heroine) must have a problem of some kind. She may, in fact, have two problems: a practical one, such as finding herself in a foreign land with no money and no means of getting back to England and safety, and an emotional one. This could be something on the lines of having lost her capacity for trusting men because of a past experience, or believing herself to be frigid and so shunning all contact with the opposite sex. (The hero, of course, will be the one to finally restore her to normality through his love: an up-dated version of *Sleeping Beauty*.)

In a novel of mine, *Sweet Revenge,* the heroine has been orphaned and made homeless by someone pulling out of a business deal with her father who, being ruined as a consequence, suffered a fatal heart attack. Finding herself alone and penniless, she determines to track down the man she believes responsible for her father's death. Needless to say, he turns out to be the hero who, unknowingly, gives her a job and a home. She, having fallen in love with him, then learns the truth but abjures revenge when presented with the opportunity. After a number of misunderstandings, all ends happily.

The days of heroines being forced to take jobs as governesses or companions to elderly ladies are out: mostly, they have satisfying careers which are usually a bit more out of the ordinary than that of secretary. I've read romantic novels where the heroines were deep-sea divers, surveyors, pilots, successful musicians, hoteliers, painters and stage-managers. Provided you are either familiar with every aspect of that profession or can research it thoroughly, it will add an extra dimension to your story.

But, whoever and whatever she is, never lose sight of the fact that the reader will want to identify with her and so, although basically she will be a thoroughly nice girl, a touch of glamour will have a definite appeal. After all, even Cinderella was a princess in disguise.

HERO

Next in importance is the hero with whom the heroine and the reader (and definitely yourself also) will fall in love. Look at some of those who have gone down into literary history as archetypes: Mr Rochester, Mr Darcy, Maximilian de Winter and Rhett Butler. Brooding and dynamic, exuding animal magnetism, sexuality and power but each hiding a caring, vulnerable side to his nature beneath a tough exterior, and the first three having little reason to trust women. Remember Rhett Butler's dramatic words to Scarlet O'Hara: 'If I wanted you, no lock would keep me out.' Can any woman read those words without getting goosepimples?

You must also know a good deal about him before you start to write. What is his background? Did he inherit wealth or acquire it by hard work? If the former, he mustn't be a playboy but have a responsible and hard-working attitude to his inheritance. What has made him the mature man he clearly is?

He will probably be in his mid-30s and successful in his chosen career. Tall, dark heroes still seem to be the most popular though there has been the occasional blond or redhaired one. His name must reflect his personality and, as you'll gather from glancing through some current romances, is often short and tough-sounding: Luke, Jake, Brett, Grant, for example, if he is English. Of course, he may well be foreign, if your book is set abroad, in which case his name will be suitably different: Philippe, Ricardo, Carlos, Andreas and so on.

He will be lithely built with the sinewy grace and strength of a wild predatory animal, with a fine head of hair (no paunches or bald pates will do) and is often likened, in the heroine's eyes, to a wild creature of the jungle, jaguar, tiger or panther or, perhaps, to a bird of prey – a hawk or eagle. These similes create an instant picture in the reader's mind of a powerful, exciting, primitive man who will be tamed, ultimately, by the heroine.

Some writers cut out pictures of a film star or male model, if he fits their image of a romantic hero, and pin them up beside their desk so they have a constant reminder of what he looks like.

You must give him human quirks and frailties though, in order to make him three-dimensional. I once had a novel rejected on the grounds that my hero was a 'too stereotypical Greek tycoon' so I had to find a way of making him more believable.

Whilst you must create a strong, sexually-attractive hero (the macho, brutal type is as defunct today, thank goodness, as is the submissive heroine), he must be an 'alpha' man, to use the current jargon, and not a wimp. Remember he is the stuff that dreams are made of.

SETTING/BACKGROUND

After your two main characters, this is next in importance and, indeed, it may be what sparked the story off, in the first place. It is against this backcloth, which plays an integral part in the tale, that their relationship will begin and develop. If you've been on holiday to somewhere exotic, you could set your story there to give it an added appeal to British readers. But don't forget that locations in the UK such as Devon, Cornwall, the Lake District and the Highlands of Scotland, have an in-built romance to foreign readers, Americans in particular.

Although it helps to write about places you actually know, it is quite possible to use one you've never been to provided you do sufficient research. I know two top romantic novelists who frequently use far-flung exciting-sounding countries such as Brazil, Mexico and Peru without ever having set foot in them. But they've researched the topography, customs, culture and life-style of the inhabitants meticulously so that it is hard to believe they don't know them intimately from first-hand.

You can sometimes find beautifully illustrated guide books remaindered in cut-price book shops, and mid-season sales often yield half-price bargains of well-known guides. Then there are travel agents' brochures, TV documentaries and films. Even if you have actually spent a holiday in, say, Greece, you would be wise to refresh your memory by looking again at your photographs, especially transparencies, and checking on details.

Your setting will largely dictate your plot because your two main characters must be part of it, naturally, and not just superimposed on a scenic backcloth. If you are using a foreign setting, for instance, even though your hero is sophisticated and cosmopolitan, his actions and reactions will be quite different to those of an English hero.

Don't lose sight of the fact that you should be creating a sense of place, not writing a travelogue, so you must make us *feel* the heat, *smell* the spices, the perfume of the exotic blossoms (smell is arguably the most evocative sense of all), *hear* the sounds of the bazaar, the street-cries, which are so different to those we are used to, and learn something of the geography, history, legends and customs of the country.

PLOT STRUCTURE

Now that you've established your hero and heroine and provided them with an interesting, romantic or exotic location in which to fall in love, you have to set the story in motion. You must now consider that vital factor in any type of fiction – conflict. As we've already discussed this in some detail (pp. 39-40), let's look at how we can use it to create interest in a romance.

There are two kinds of conflict – internal and external – and you should ensure you have both in your story. The interest in any work of fiction will be heightened, and the tension increased, if you remember this basic rule. For example, in a story of mine, the stables are on fire and the heroine has to battle against it to release the horses (external conflict). But, because she almost lost her life in one, she is exceptionally afraid of fire so an internal battle also rages between her desire to flee to safety and her love for the animals.

There will also be the obvious clashes between hero and heroine, the result of misunderstandings, as they are drawn together, then pulled apart as if by a piece of invisible elastic. But these

126

must be believable and arise logically as the story progresses. To give an example from another story of mine: hero is already suspicious about heroine's motives for turning up 'out of the blue' to see his sick, wealthy father. When he catches her coming out of his father's bedroom, late at night, there is an explosive confrontation and the conflict between them escalates. In fact, she had gone there for a very understandable reason – to seek comfort and reassurance from the man who, unknown to the hero, wants to adopt her as his legal daughter.

Conflict will also stem from other characters (in particular from the 'other man' and 'other woman' who so frequently appear in romantic novels) because of the misunderstandings they cause.

Plot will invariably spring from character although, most likely, characters and the setting will fuse in your mind, resulting in the basic plot being born almost by osmosis. In that sense, it is impossible to separate the three. But, at that point, you will only have your basic outline which then needs to be filled in so that you have a complete framework on which to build. Bear in mind that the average romance has ten chapters. This can vary but, when you are beginning, it will be easier to stick to the usual ten, each of roughly equal length, the actual word count depending on the publisher aimed at.

Although you will hear some writers say they don't plot their story in advance, they will probably be fairly experienced. The consensus of opinion is that it is wiser to do so to make sure you have a good idea of the direction you are taking. Personally, I like to outline chapter by chapter so that I can see how the conflict will build up in a roller-coaster effect as the book moves towards its climax. However, as always, each writer must find his/her own best method of working.

An arresting, intriguing opening is essential. It could be a line of dialogue with dramatic impact; a short descriptive passage that hints at storms ahead, emotional as well as weatherwise; an unexpected initial confrontation with the hero. It is essential to plunge your heroine into a believable but difficult situation in the first 350 words. Her life, her entire world has been or is about to be turned upside down and, with the entrance of the hero, will never be the same again. (This is usually their first encounter though sometimes a second, following a period of years during which they haven't seen each other.)

Have your heroine desperately wanting something of importance to her well-being *and doing something about getting it.* Following on that, through her own foolishness, even her good intentions perhaps, and through misunderstandings, a situation develops whereby although hero and heroine are clearly attracted to each other and the reader knows they are falling in love, each believes the worst of the other. This produces the push/pull scenario which makes up a romantic novel.

Your hero should come into the action early, preferably on the first page if you can stage-manage it realistically, even if it is only by a mention of his name:

> 'Who does Luke Ballam think he is – God?' Catriona demanded, eyes flashing.

No need to spell out that Luke is the hero and that, from the opening sentence, trouble is brewing between them.

Chapter 1 should explain who, what and where the heroine is and what her predicament is. You may need a flashback to indicate this but, if so, keep it brief. There is no need to give great chunks of her background at this point; it will hold up the story. Further information can be fed in later, bit by bit. In chapters 2 and 3, the situation between them ferments, it boils up in chapter 4 to 7 or 8, at the end of which comes the climax or highest point in the story. After that, you should be on a downwards curve ready to enter the home straight when everything will be resolved.

If you build in one major problem and several minor ones, even though the latter will gradually be resolved throughout the book, the major one will remain until the end, thus keeping up the tension until the final heart-throbbing resolution. The ending naturally, it hardly needs to be said, must be a happy one, resulting either in marriage or the promise of it or, if they are married already, in the clearing away of all obstacles, enabling them to live happily ever after together from then on. And, last but not least, it must create in the reader a rosy glow of satisfaction that all's right with a world in which romance still blossoms.

Whilst you have to invent ways in which to keep your hero and heroine together, avoid cliché situations such as broken ankles. Try to come up with something fresh and original. Each chapter, too, will have a shape in which it rises to a peak, a tiny climax, and then slopes down a little, ending with a 'hook' to impel the reader to read on. One such that is regularly used, successfully, is for the heroine to finally realise she is irrevocably in love with a man whom she cannot possibly have for some reason. Maybe because he despises her or she him; maybe she thinks he is committed to someone else; or for some other plausible and, hopefully, original reason you can come up with.

To analyse structure, break down several published novels, chapter by chapter, outlining in a sentence or two the main action of each chapter.

A word about pace. It should be brisk and a high proportion of dialogue will help move the story along rapidly. Narrative reduces pace, so keep it down to small doses. Use the heroine's thoughts and feelings where possible, rather than straight narrative.

LOVE SCENES

It goes without saying that you can't have a romance without love scenes. Fashions change, in this respect, as with everything else and the 'closing of the bedroom door' behind the lovers is no longer either necessary or desirable. You are writing a love story for modern readers whose knowledge of sex and familiarity with its being openly discussed has expanded dramatically over the past few decades. However, you should never force yourself to write anything that makes you feel uncomfortable.

Many writers of romance have gimmicks to help put them in the right mood for writing love scenes, such as putting on sexy music, wearing a glamorous dress, dabbing on expensive perfume, lowering the lights and so on. In effect, do whatever is necessary to create a romantic ambiance in which to write a powerful and tender love scene. But let sensual be the key-note rather than explicit sex. This will involve making use of the senses: 'His tanned fingers scarcely touched her bare arm yet, to Katrina, it seemed that their imprint had seared her flesh, branding her his forever.' Evoke the manly tag of your hero's skin; the deep tone of his voice; the brilliant cobalt of his eyes softening to the blue of a summer sky as he held her in his arms.

Sibilants help create a sensual mood for the reader: sexy, silky, smooth, sinewy, sinuous and so on. Make a list of similar words and put them to good use.

SUMMARY OF INGREDIENTS FOR A SUCCESSFUL CATEGORY ROMANCE

1   A likeable, spunky heroine.

2   A strong, dynamic, sexually-attractive hero in a high-powered job.

3   An interesting, romantic and/or exotic setting.

4   An original but credible situation which allows plenty of scope for the development of the plot, with the necessary conflict and in which the hero and heroine will be kept together yet apart until the end.

5   All your skill as a writer to conjure up for your reader this wonderful fantasy world into which she can escape for a little while.

6   A happy-ever-after ending that will leave your reader with a warm glow of content.

NOTES OF INTEREST

The Romantic Novelists' Association (RNA) was formed in 1960 with its avowed aim 'to use all the means in its power, individually and collectively, to raise the prestige of Romantic Authorship.' It has a membership of around 500 plus Associate Members (publishers, editors, literary agents, etc.) and Probationary Members who, as yet, have not had a romantic novel published.

The RNA has a quarterly journal and two annual awards for romantic fiction. These have changed slightly, recently, and the major one is now known as The Boots' Romantic Novel of the Year Award (sponsored by Boots) while the second, open to Probationary Members only, comes under the New Writers' Scheme but is still known as the Netta Muskett Award.

Application form and information re. fees etc. are obtainable from The Hon. Treasurer, Mrs Marina Oliver, Half Hidden, West Lane, Nr Princes Risborough, Bucks HP17 9PF. (enclosing S.A.E.).

Guidelines are available from many romantic-novel publishers, including Robert Hale and Mills & Boon. The latter have produced a cassette, *And Then He Kissed Her*, which is obtainable from Mills & Boon Reader Service, Freepost P.O. Box 236, Croydon, Surrey CR9 9EL.

Top Tip from Sara Craven

Author of more than 40 novels for Mills & Boon.

Getting yourself out of the slush-pile

Firstly, if you're writing solely for the money and you think a predominantly women's market is easy – forget it. Sincerity is the keyword if you are to succeed where so many others have failed. You are writing about the secret fantasy world of women and your reader needs to identify with your heroine who must be a real woman with real feelings. You must become her and fall in love with the hero, also.

Basically, the story is about a man and a woman who are made whole by each other. Its driving force is their relationship and emotional depth is needed to carry this on throughout its length.

The first page is of vital importance, the book starting at a moment of crisis, a turning point in the heroine's life which will draw the reader into the story. Hero and heroine must be kept apart by both internal and external conflict and the ideal book maintains a balance between these. But it is her internal conflict, as she fights her growing awareness of, and desire for, the hero, that will provide the most mileage.

She is the 'nice girl next door' while he should have a strongly sexual attraction. If they dislike each other on sight, make sure there is a good reason for it. Get yourself into the right mood for creating your love scenes and don't try to make them 'steamy' if it offends your sensibilities.

Finally, if you become deeply involved in this developing relationship, you will be well on the way to success in this demanding but rewarding field of romance.

Science fiction

Science fiction is a very specialised type of fiction which you are likely to love (in which case you may wish to try writing it) or loathe. Many would-be science fiction writers, perhaps because they have not fully understood the genre, think that it merely consists of creating an imaginary planet in a galactic world, populating it with strange creatures from space and using high-tech terminology (or inventing some) and that will suffice. It will not, of course.

One of the biggest hurdles in writing for this genre is probably getting across background information, which readers must have and understand in order to make sense of the story, without holding up the narrative with clumsy chunks of exposition. Despite its alien landscape, science fiction must contain all the same elements as any other kind of fiction. It needs conflict (man against man or himself as well as the more obvious man against his environment). It needs structure, with the main character resolving his own problem.

Although you are creating a fantasy world, it must have its own reality and its characters must be believable, with normal reactions, and motivated by emotions we can recognise, such as jealousy, anger, love, loyalty and so on. The way of life of their society must be shown in action. This can only be done through believable and interesting characters.

Asimov Science Fiction Magazine, probably the best known in its genre and, according to its editor, very accessible to new writers, has apparently bought some of its best stories from people who had never sold a story before. Its guidelines stress that the emphasis should be on the characters rather than on the science or the setting: 'We look for change, growth or development in some respect of the characters' lives'.

Interzone is, to date, the only science fiction and fantasy magazine in the UK and they encourage new writers of a wide range of fiction within this genre. With regular contributors of the calibre of J. G. Ballard, their standard is high. But who said anything would do for Sci-fi? It won't – and, like any other genre fiction, its particular parameters need to be studied and understood.

Science fiction guidelines may be obtained by writing to:
Asimov Science Fiction Magazine, 380 Lexington Avenue, New York 10017, USA and (enclosing a SAE) to *Interzone*, 124 Osborne Road, Brighton BN1 6LU.

The short story

...[it] follows, step by step, the main idea.

Sean O'Faolain, *The Short Story*

A brief brilliant insight into a situation and the people involved in it.

H. E. Bates

Firstly, let's consider what a short story is and is not. According to Frank O'Connor, a classic short story writer, 'The short story...springs from the heart of a situation rather than mounts up to and explains it.'

We might, perhaps, simply say that it is just a short piece of fiction. We can say, definitely, that it is not a anecdote, that it is not a character sketch or a 'slice of life', although it may well have sprung from any one of these. And, although the genre is called the 'short story', how long is short? That question is often put to creative writing teachers. Unfortunately, the answer – that it should always find its own length – must sound unsatisfactory. That can be qualified by adding that, today, the average saleable length is likely to be between 2,000 and 4,000 words, depending on the market. One of only 1000 words (most likely with a 'twist' ending) is known as a 'short short'. Anything less than that would be very difficult to write and almost impossible to sell unless for a very specific market, whilst one of more than 5000 words would have few commercial outlets.

Expanding that first definition, then, we might go on to say that it is a piece of fiction which will be satisfactorily concluded within a length of 1000 to 5000 words.

The next point to consider – and the most important, I feel – is whose story is it that you propose telling? It is vital that you identify this before you start because it will be about *one* person wanting something: to achieve a goal or solve a problem. It may be concrete or abstract (a new hat for a wedding; the attentions of a particular young man or regaining a lost good name, for example) but it must be of great significance to that person. And there must be obstacles in her path preventing her attaining it or solving it.

Note I stress one character, not two or more, even though there will probably be others involved. Sometimes, a student in class will start to outline a story, saying, for example: 'It's about a young couple who want a baby and...' Here I stop him and ask: 'But whose story is it?', and then explain that it must be *one* person's only because the focus of the short story is narrow. It turns a spotlight on the particular hope, dream, desire of a single character at one moment in time.

Having established that it is the young wife's story (because it is she who most longs for a baby) and that she has just come back from the doctor's where she has learned that she is infertile and that nothing more can be done, we must ask one more question: where will the action of the story take place? This sometimes meets with raised eyebrows because does it matter where? Yes, it does.

Suppose that, desolate at the prospect of never becoming a mother, she agrees to go with her husband on a trek around the world, something he'd wanted to do but which she'd refused to agree to previously. If the author now takes them on their adventures over the next couple of years, the story breaks down again because the action is spread over a long time span and a wide location.

This example illustrates the relevance of the Greek Unities of Time, Place and Action, so called because they were handed down to us by Aristotle in his *Poetics*, a treatise which deals with Greek theatre. Early exponents of the short story realised that observing these unities gave it the tight structure it demanded.

The Unity of Time is best observed in terms of a short time span (an hour, a day or a week, maybe) between the opening and closing scenes. We know that life has gone on up to that point and that it will continue afterwards but we are only interested in that brief intervening period.

The Unity of Place means setting the action of the story in one location only. This unity can be dispensed with provided it doesn't unbalance the story, which would happen if it took place in several countries or locations but, by beginning and ending the story in the same place, unity is preserved. Any minor changes between the beginning and the ending will therefore not upset the unity of place.

The Unity of Action is the action of the one person who, desperately wanting something, faces a number of obstacles in his attempt to obtain it.

Our definition has now expanded to read: A short piece of fiction, probably between 1000 and 5000 words in length, dealing with a single incident in the life of one person and taking place during a short space of time and preferably starting and ending in one location.

If we use the analogy of the camera, we can think of the snapshot, where the focus is on one person in one setting. And when, in years to come, we look at the snapshot again, we recall that person, that particular place and what was happening at that particular moment: Mary's graduation ceremony, for instance. We have highlighted Mary on that day in 1988 at X University when she received her degree, a moment in time which was especially significant to her because, despite all the problems – the short spell in hospital, the death of a friend, the losing of her notes – she achieved her ambition which was captured by that snapshot.

The keyword, here, is 'significant'. Henry James said that 'Life is all inclusion and confusion. Art is all discrimination and selection.' It is the selection of the significant details that is all-important in the short story: there is no room for anything else.

Many years ago, when I was beginning to write, Alexander Cordell gave a memorable talk to the writers' circle to which I belonged. He gave us a quotation which he said he kept on his desk so that it was always in front of him. I reproduce for you, here, those same words, penned by the man who is regarded by many as being the father of the modern short story, Edgar Allen Poe.

A skilful artist has constructed a tale. If wise, he has not fashioned his thoughts to accommodate his incidents; but having conceived with deliberate care a certain unique or single effect to be brought out, he then invents such incidents – he then contrives such effects as may best aid him in establishing this preconceived effect. If his very initial sentence tends not to the outbringing of this effect, then he has failed in his first step. In the whole composition there should be no word written of which the tendency, direct or indirect, is not to the pre-established design.

Now, let's talk about structure in terms everyone has heard of: a beginning, a middle and an end.

THE BEGINNING

1   This should introduce the main character (the person whose story it is should be the first to be named).

2   It should set the tone (e.g. humorous, sad, romantic, horror, ghost or mystery).

3   It should disclose the problem to be solved.

4   It should show the setting or background against which the action will take place (e.g. country cottage, Australian outback, old people's home).

THE MIDDLE

This will show the main character's struggles against the obstacles in his path until the climax is reached.

THE END

This will be the *satisfying* conclusion following the climax, a conclusion that is right for it. It might not be a happy one but it must leave the reader feeling that no other would have done. It must be brought about by the MC's own efforts, not by coincidence or through the efforts of someone else; nor in that infuriating and totally unacceptable way of having it turn out to have been only a dream after all. And the MC should have changed, matured, learned a little more about life.

At this point, you are probably thinking this seems incredibly complex for a piece of fiction that is only a few thousand words long – and you would be right. However, the short story is generally considered to be, next to poetry, the most precise and difficult form of writing. Indeed, Truman Capote called it 'the most difficult and disciplining form of prose writing extant'. It doesn't allow the same sprawling scope as the novel but it is probably the best form of apprenticeship any writer can have in learning his craft.

We might now consider where stories spring from. Invariably, I think, they spring from character. They might germinate from an incident told you by someone, from a newspaper item, from something you observed but, instantly, a figure will appear in your mind and you will 'see' an old man, a pretty young woman or a tall, bronzed sailor, and begin to weave your story in your head.

To give an example: many years ago, day after day, summer and winter, an elderly man used to stand in the doorway of a large department store clad in old trousers and a string vest. Beside him lay an iron barbell which he would lift, occasionally, and a board on which were displayed photographs showing him as a young man wearing the leopard-skin costume of a circus strongman. Intrigued by this sad figure, obviously clinging to past glory when he'd been in the limelight of the sawdust ring, I asked myself what had happened to change him into this wreck of a man reduced virtually to begging. I also asked that vital word – why? A writer's instincts set to work and I wrote one of my first-ever published stories. I called it *Alberto The Great*, and I will use it here to illustrate plot-building.

BEGINNING

Opening scene and problem shown. Albert, once billed as Alberto The Great, strongest man in the world, stares into a cracked mirror and sees a flabby, ageing figure. He then glances at a picture showing him twenty years before in leopard skin, muscles rippling, legs apart as he demonstrates his strength. Remembering his past glory he wishes he could make a come-back but, deep down, knows it's too late.

MIDDLE

He's now at his position as doorman outside a large city store when a nearby partly-demolished building collapses. A woman shrieks that her child is trapped beneath the rubble and begs someone in the crowd of onlookers (which includes Albert) to help. For a moment Albert is tempted to go to her aid.

FIRST OBSTACLE/COMPLICATION

Then he remembers the past, how his lovely wife, Gina the acrobat, had left him for the circus juggler. How he had begun to drink, his performance suffering until, on that last terrible night, his act had been so bad that he had been given the slow handclap. That had finished him – so how could he risk another humiliation?

SECOND OBSTACLE

The child is screaming; the woman weeps in despair and pleads for someone to help as she vainly struggles to free the child – and another piece of masonry crashes down. Long before the fire brigade arrives with proper equipment, the child might be dead – but no one can possible lift that coping stone. But Albert knows how it could be done – he has learned many tricks in his circus days.

THIRD OBSTACLE (THE CLIMAX)

As he hesitates once again, a wall sways dangerously, the mother screams – and he makes his decision.

THE ENDING

Using an iron bar lying on the site, he levers the huge stone until he can begin to slide his shoulders beneath it, taking its weight enough to allow the child to wriggle free. The crowd cheers, the fire-engine's bell is heard in the distance but Albert cannot hold the coping up any longer and it falls, crushing him beneath. But, even as the stone falls, he is smiling at the resounding applause for Alberto The Great.

A sad ending? No, because Albert got what he most wanted – a glorious come-back, wiping out the shame of his last performance. He died with a smile on his face.

I hope this demonstrates how, from the initial germ of an idea based on a real character, I built up my own version of his life-story, of his problem (in his case, a goal), of the obstacles preventing his solving it and how, at the 'blackest moment', the climax, he brings about the resolution *by his own efforts*.

Remembering that the word 'crisis' means decision and that 'climax' means ladder should help you with understanding construction. And it is in that 'blackest moment' of the short story that the seed of the conclusion is contained. Bruce Pattison, in his book *Good English*, said of the climax: 'It must be a moment of dramatic tension, a climax for which the rest of the story prepares; for the climax is the justification for the story's existence.' For this reason, I believe it is imperative to know the ending before you begin. I like to use the analogy of a journey. A novel is akin to setting off on a fortnight's holiday. You intend going to the Highlands of Scotland but if, *en route*, you are entranced by the Cumbrian scenery, you can spare a day or so to stop and explore. However, if you are only on a day-trip somewhere, you just haven't time to break your journey.

Having established your main character's problem or goal, if he then has to overcome one obstacle only before he resolves it, there is little time in which to build up the tension necessary to maintain the reader's interest. If there are two obstacles, his interest will be more fully aroused. If there are three or more, hopefully, he will be rivetted and unable to put the story down until he knows how it ends. But each successive step or obstacle must grow in intensity until the climax is reached, followed swiftly by the dénouement. Any temptation to add anything extra which would create an anti-climax must be avoided.

I firmly believe it is vital to spend sufficient time in thinking through a story, in planning its development in terms of crises increasing in scale of intensity. (Even the more 'literary' ones are structured thus although it may not be so apparent at first glance.) In this connection, I will quote Edith Ronald Mirrielees (in whose creative writing class John Steinbeck began studying his craft). In her book *Story Writing*, discussing certain weaknesses she has found, she says they come usually 'from the author's not having given the story enough thought before it was put on paper.'

Because a student once said to me in rather disparaging tones: 'But that's just like painting by numbers', referring to my remarks on structure, I'd like to stress that it most definitely is not. This concept of shape and form applies to all the arts and herein lies the essential difference between being willing to accept that one is learning a craft and believing that it just happens by accident. In the introduction to her book, Mirrielees aptly puts it thus:

> As for the amateur, his difficulty is that his work, once on the page, hardens as cement hardens and can no more be changed. When he has learned to change it, to consider it in this light, to consider it in that, to hold the subject warm in his affections at the same time that his mind appraises the form – when that time comes, he is no longer an amateur.

I would ask you to reflect on those words of wisdom when considering the short story form.

Finally, I will leave you with the following definition of the short story. It is a short piece of fiction, usually between 1000 and 5000 words in length, highlighting a single incident in the life of the main character and involving him in overcoming several obstacles before the resolution, by his own efforts, thus bringing about a change in his outlook on life.

ANALYSING SHORT STORIES

Whilst engaged upon writing this book, I was on a Writer's Holiday in South Wales and I overheard someone say in plaintive tones: 'We're always being told to analyse stories but no one ever tells us how.' I made a mental note to include it in this *A to Z* for all those with the same plea.

When you are setting out to try to write short stories, whether for a particular magazine or not, it will pay dividends if you analyse published stories critically, virtually taking them apart bit by bit to see what made them work and why they were accepted. I would suggest you choose those you enjoyed on a first reading, although you can also learn a lot from finding out why you didn't enjoy others. Having read and enjoyed the story once, take a sheet of paper and make a list of questions to ask as you start to re-read, this time analytically.

1   Who is the main character (MC)? In a short story, this is always the first person to be named. And is the story told in the first or third person?

2   What is the MC's sex, age, socio-economic group?

3   How many other characters are involved in the story and who are they?

4   What is the tone/type/mood of the story? Is it nostalgic,

light-hearted, sad, romantic, a mystery, ghost or horror tale? This should be clear from the beginning.

5   When is the story taking place – present-day to further back in time? If the latter, it will indicate that that particular magazine likes period or historical fiction.

6   What is the proportion of dialogue to narrative?

7   What is the MC's problem or goal? This should be clear in the first few paragraphs.

8   What is the initial crisis that sets the story in motion? It will be close to the opening and will plunge the MC into it, midstream, so to speak.

9   What is the MC's reaction to this crisis and how does he/she attempt to resolve it? What is the effect of this attempt? In some way, it should have made things worse, i.e. brought about another crisis.

10   How does the MC deal with this further crisis or obstacle?

11   List any further crises in the story, ending with the final one, the climax or 'blackest moment' out of which will come the resolution.

12   Did the ending satisfy you? If not, why not? Perhaps you felt it was weak, as if the writer didn't really know how to end it and so allowed it to tail off, leaving you feeling cheated. Or did it end (horror of horrors!) with a coincidence which solved the MC's problem?

Once you have stripped a story to its bare bones, you should have some idea of why it appealed to an editor and so was accepted. Even if you didn't much like it, it will be helpful to understand why not.

Studying the anatomy of a work of fiction is always time well spent because it is lack of structure that makes so many potentially good stories fail. Imagine making a dress or building a set of bookshelves without using a pattern, taking measurements or making a drawing first. The chances are that they wouldn't fit.

Show, don't tell

This is a phrase you will have heard many times if you belong to any kind of writing group, but just how to accomplish it may still be eluding you. It is also known as 'indirect exposition'. Whichever term you use, it simply means showing your characters in action rather than narrating what is happening to them. It creates immediacy, thus bringing the scene to life, and will automatically involve the use of dialogue and/or thoughts.

It will probably help if you think of each 'scene' of your story as a unit of action that is taking place in front of you just as if it were a stage play. And, just as if it were taking place on a stage, it should move the story forwards a little, or show another facet of your character and arouse some emotion in your reader.

No piece of fiction that is pure narrative will 'leap off the page' at the reader, which isn't to say that narrative is never needed. The secret is to decide which particular portions of a story are especially important and then make a scene of them, that is – *show* them taking place, leaving narrative for bridging passages or for where you merely want to hurry the reader forward into the next slice of action.

Here is a short example of how *not* to write a scene because it is utterly static:

> Harry Potterton was taking his dog, Benjy, for his evening walk in the park when he noticed the thin figure of a youth skulking near the undergrowth. He wondered if he should tell the park attendant or just ignore it and, in the end, decided it was none of his business, called the dog to heel and went on walking.

The following is one way of writing the same scene using indirect exposition:

> It was Benjy's barking, when they were out for their evening

walk, that drew Harry Potterton's attention to the undergrowth at the edge of the park. 'Benjy, come here boy,' he called in what he hoped was a commanding voice. But the dog stayed where he was, refusing to budge. And then Harry saw the thin skulking figure of a youth. 'Now just what's he up to?'he asked himself, irritably, and glanced round to see if there was any sign of the park attendant. There wasn't so, with a sharp,'Benjy, come', he called the dog to heel and walked swiftly on.

The second example gives you the same information but tells you a little more about Harry Potterton. Reading that he speaks in what he hopes is a commanding voice, we know that he isn't an authoritative sort of person but is merely trying to give the impression that he is. Nor is he decisive: he doesn't know what to do about the suspicious youth. His annoyance shows he feels he ought to do something about it but,true to character, he doesn't.

Thus the reader is actively involved in the scene, interpreting the action as he 'watches' it.

All this might seem obvious, yet many beginners write long tracts of stultifying narrative without realising their mistake. The following passage is typical of part of a beginner's story. You might like to re-write it as an exercise:

John Hamlin didn't feel sleepy, that night, so he decided to go for a walk instead of going to bed. Telling his wife he wouldn't be long, he set off in the direction of the woods at the edge of the village. He heard the clock chime midnight as he approached a dense copse of tall trees, their branches silvered in the moonlight. Suddenly he felt scared and began to wonder what on earth he was doing there when he could have been at home in his cosy bed next to the warm body of his wife.

Hearing a rustle close beside him, he turned with a start, catching a glimpse of a lithe low shape silhouetted in a small clearing before it disappeared into the darkness. Shivering with fright, John thought that maybe he should turn and

147

hurry back the way he'd come but then he pulled him-self together and stoutly carried on, the pathway ahead illuminated by the full moon riding high in the sky.

You might even use this as a springboard for a short story: even if a hundred of you use it, you'll all come up with one that is entirely different.

Style

Proper words in proper places make the true definition of a style.

Jonathan Swift

Good writers are those who keep the language efficient.

Ezra Pound

Style is a much-bandied literary term which it is not easy to define. It is the writer's own stamp, reflecting his personality, but which may need to be modified, depending upon the type of writing on which he is engaged. For instance, when setting out to write this book, I knew I wanted a chatty, 'me talking to you' style. I would not have felt comfortable attempting an erudite approach; nor would I have been reaching the audience at which I was aiming.

Every writer, however, is bound to be influenced by those he admires and, consciously or unconsciously, will attempt a similar style at first – just as any artist, when learning his craft, observes the techniques used so effectively by the masters. I think one of the commonest mistakes made by beginners, though, is striving for what they perceive as a 'literary' style. They usually end up with a 'flowery' prose, littered with adjectives and words that aren't exactly right, and which is merely pretentious. A writer whose style is genuinely 'literary' (e.g. Lawrence Durrell, Iris Murdoch) will tend to use a wide range of vocabulary and, in all probability, to allude to classical literature and the arts in general. Their choice of words, their control of structure, their humour are all inevitably influenced by their reading (hence 'literary'); but nonetheless their style is authentically original, not assumed. They are not pretentious, but anyone striving to adopt a literary style might well end up seeming so.

Do not, however, confuse 'literary' with 'literate'. Every writer can safely strive to be literate and, in this connection, there are guidelines to what is generally considered to be good style.

Chekhov said that the essence of style is simplicity, yet some writers, such as those mentioned above, are successful with prose that is anything but simple. For most of us, however, I feel it is wise to pay heed to his advice.

George Orwell also laid down some 'rules' (though I think he may have 'borrowed' them from Fowler's *The King's English* and adapted them slightly). These are, in brief:

1   Never use a metaphor, simile or other figure of speech which you are used to seeing in print.

2   Never use a long word where a short one will do.

3   If it's possible to cut out a word, do so.

4   Never use the passive voice when you can use the active. ('The sight of it jolted him into action' rather than 'He was jolted into action by the sight of it.')

5   Never use jargon or foreign phrases if you can find an English equivalent.

6   Break any of these rules, if necessary.

Perhaps it is this last that proves the rules.

Orwell also maintained that clear thinking is the key to clear writing – and clarity, after all, is what we should be striving for, always. He said that 'a scrupulous writer in every sentence that he writes will ask himself at least four questions: 'What am I trying to say? What words will express it? What image or idiom will make it clearer? Is this image fresh enough to have an effect?' Then perhaps two more: 'Could I put it more shortly? Have I said anything that is avoidably ugly?'

The two most important words are, I suggest, 'clearer' and 'fresh'. And we should never forget that good writers work hard at their craft and that those phrases, paragraphs and pages which we find so clear and fresh were the result of much thought and effort.

Nothing labels the amateur more immediately than the use of clichés and those hackneyed media phrases: 'tip of the iceberg' (how frequently that is used to convey the impression of an enormous problem that is only just surfacing); 'at this point in time'; 'militate against'. These are merely crutches for the lazy to lean upon. The only time you should use them is when you put them into the mouths of characters who would speak thus. (Incidentally, isn't it fascinating to discover the origins of familiar words and phrases? '*Cliché*', for instance, comes from the French meaning a printer's stereotype plate which was kept ready for instant insertion. '*Hackneyed*' is derived from the hackney carriage of old which used to ply for hire and whose horses were usually worn out.

Avoid, too, the over-lavish use of adjectives. An adjective describes a noun and has its legitimate place in our language, but be selective and don't use one, or more, with almost every noun: the effect you are trying to create is likely to be lessened if you do.

Similarly, be sparing with your use of adverbs (which qualify a verb and tend to weaken it), preferring whenever possible to choose a strong active verb that conveys the same meaning. For example: 'He devoured his food' rather than 'he ate voraciously'; 'she dawdled/ambled' instead of 'she proceeded slowly'; 'her hands trembled', not 'her hands shook nervously'. Again, it isn't a question of omitting them completely but rather of using them judiciously and not seeing them as an easy option. (They shriek 'amateur' if they appear too often in a piece of writing.)

Another 'don't'. Don't use abstract words such as 'beautiful', 'passion', 'feelings'. Be specific and say in what way something is beautiful or exactly how someone is feeling. Axe those 'purple passages' which we all fall in love with, from time to time. Avoid circumlocutions. If your character is rolling drunk, say so, not that he is in 'a state of intoxication'.

Watch out for mistakes in syntax. It can be quite amusing to spot them when they turn up in newsprint, as they all too often do. Geoffrey Ashe in *The Art of Writing Made Simple*, published by Heinemann, 1972, gives the following exaggerated examples to make the point:

If your baby does not thrive on raw milk, boil it.
Alsatian dog for sale. Eats anything. Very fond of children.

Similarly, avoid phrases like: 'Her eyes were glued to the paper in front of her.' Painful!

Search for fresh imagery. Here is a sentence from Dylan Thomas's *Daydreams and Nightmares*. 'The over-filled bowl of his pipe smouldered among his whiskers like a little burning hayrick on a stick.' How evocative those words are; what a vivid picture they conjure up in the mind and how they illustrate Orwell's stricture that: 'A newly-invented metaphor assists thought by evoking a visual image.'

Don't pepper your pages with exclamation marks or dashes or rows of dots to indicate the omission of words. Beware too of complicated sentence structures of the 'Backwards ran the sentence until reeled the mind' type.

Listen to the rhythm of your sentences. If they don't flow and are not easy on the ear, try cutting out words or repositioning them. This can make all the difference to the way your work sounds.

Regarding the vexed question of the split infinitive (where an adverb comes between 'to' and the verb, e.g. 'he started to carefully scrub...'), according to Fowler's *Modern English Usage*, although it is not desirable in itself it is preferable to ambiguity and to patent artificiality.

Using the active voice rather than the passive usually helps to strengthen a piece of writing although you may wish to use the latter in order to vary the pace a little on occasions.

Don't use mixed metaphors. For example: 'He was always

burying his head in the sand and riding rough shod over every-one.' 'He was a tower of strength as he forged ahead.'

Finally, never forget that words are the tools with which a writer has to work so take pains to use them to their full advantage. And, to sum up, back to Chekhov: 'The essence of good style is simplicity.' Keep that in mind and you'll avoid most of the pitfalls mentioned.

Suspense

Suspense, my dictionary states, is a 'state of uncertainty, doubt or apprehensive expectation or waiting'. It is that element in a story that keeps the reader turning the page. It is what makes a child wriggle on the seat of its chair, eyes wide and expectant, and whisper: 'Go on, what happens next?' It is the tool that Scheherazade used to such effect, stringing out her tales of the Arabian Nights, finishing each instalment on what has come to be known as a 'cliff-hanger' so that the Sultan couldn't bear to have her killed because then he would never know how the story ended.

The term 'suspense' is as relevant to the romance and to the 'straight' novel as it is to the mystery, thriller or horror story. It is the essence of good story-telling. If you can learn to use it or already have an instinctive knowledge of it, once you have mastered the other necessary techniques you will have a good chance of succeeding.

When you pick up a book at bedtime intending to read just a few pages and find yourself unable to put it down, that is the book to analyse critically when you have finished it. It will be a perfect example of the magic ingredient in operation. For me *Gone With The Wind* was one such book. And a modern writer who demonstrates it perfectly, I think, is Diane Pearson whose *The Summer of the Barshinkeys* and *Csardas* kept me awake long after I should have been asleep.

Such writing doesn't just come about by accident. It is the result of much careful thought. It will have been honed and shaped during months, maybe years, of hard work so that the story is skilfully spun out to ensure the reader keeps on turning those pages. Imagine a deep-sea fisherman dexterously 'playing' a big fish, reeling out to let it think it is getting away, then reeling in just a little, creating tension on the line, and repeating this procedure until the fish is drawn close, when, with a final tightening, there is one last almighty battle, and the fish is landed. In the case of writing, the 'play' will lead to the obligatory scene, the climax, after which comes the dénouement, the last unravelling of the knot.

The words suspense and tension are complementary: indeed one cannot exist without the other. Create tension in your story and there will be suspense and vice versa. One method is to drop in clues, casually as if they are of no importance, which the astute reader will notice and will be eager to see followed up.

This is where it seems appropriate to mention Chekhov's famed 'Gun on the wall'. The great dramatist once said that, if there is a gun on the wall in the first act, it must go off in the last. In effect, you mustn't cheat your reader or audience. They are anticipating these clues as to the story's development and its ending and, when they think they've spotted one, tension begins to build up until they learn its significance. A gun on a wall promises a big bang and someone being shot and you mustn't let your reader down. This is known as foreshadowing conflict.

There are various ways of creating suspense in a story. For example, suppose when your story opens it is a beautiful summer's day. Your main character, relaxed and happy, notices a dark swirl of dust on the horizon. A rider is approaching at a furious pace. We would then be thrust into the main character's mind as he or she waits with rising anxiety to find out who it is and why they are in such a hurry.

In a well-told story or play, suspense remains such an integral part of it that, even though you may have read it or seen it several times over, it still has you on the edge of your seat, desperately hoping that, this time, the ending might be different. Is there any woman who, having read *Gone with the Wind*, doesn't re-read it longing that Scarlett O'Hara will behave differently and that Rhett won't stride away from her, at the end, but will turn back, sweep her into his arms and carry her upstairs to make up their differences once and for all? And I expect there are those who, like me, can't watch *Othello* without desperately hoping that, this time, he will see through Iago's evil machinations and will not kill Desdemona.

Part of the technique in creating suspense lies in the placing of suitable and credible obstacles in the path of the main character and forcing him or her to strive to overcome them. If each chapter of your book ends with some kind of difficulty to be faced or a cliff-hanger, even if only a minor one (and it would become monotonous if they were all on the same scale), you are unlikely to lose your reader part way through.

The use of what is sometimes called the 'time-bomb' technique is another very effective way of building suspense. Something catastrophic will occur if your main character cannot accomplish a given task within a certain time-limit. In the opera *Turandot*, for instance, the hero, Prince Caliph, has given the cruel princess till dawn to learn his name. If she succeeds, he will die. In the adventure-type story, the river is rising rapidly and, if the hero or heroine can't make it to the bank within the next hour, it will be impossible to cross and someone will be doomed to die.

Something of vital importance must be at stake to make this 'time-bomb' work. If the heroine merely wanted to go and visit a friend, the fact that the river was rising wouldn't matter at all as she could just turn back and go some other time.

Symbolism

Whether symbolism is consciously put into a work of fiction or not is debatable and, in any case, probably depends on the individual writer. However, it is an interesting subject to consider and, when you start searching for symbols in fiction, it's surprising how many you find.

They are a kind of literary shorthand. As John Steinbeck puts it in his *Journal of Novel*: 'It is a kind of psychological sign language. It is...chosen to illuminate as well as to illustrate the whole.' He mentions a scarred forehead which he will use as a kind of recurring symbol. He then asks, rhetorically, what does it mean? And answers: 'the maimed, the marked, the guilty...all such things: the imperfect.'

Did Iris Murdoch in *The Bell* deliberately make use of symbolism in allowing Dora to catch a butterfly in the opening scenes and to free it at the end of the chapter? Whether or not she did, the beautiful, delicate insect is there, trapped in a railway carriage, just as Dora is trapped in her marriage, having tried to escape but now having to return to her husband.

Think of some of the more obvious symbols and their associations. White for purity and innocence; shadows and darkness for the sinister, evil or mysterious; a house for security; scaling mountains or heights for overcoming a problem or difficulty; bees for industry; a ring denoting completeness, wholeness – the magic circle of safety.

The fury of waves beating against a rock will suggest an inner rage in the character watching them. A passage showing the show, rhythmic rise and fall of waves on the shore until they burst upon the rocks in a white foaming crescendo, if part of a love scene, should evoke sufficiently erotic images in the reader's mind to allow the actual physical description to be understated.

157

In a horror or ghost story, the sound of a door creaking on its hinges, maybe on a bright summer's day, gives the reader a mental nudge to watch out because something's going to happen soon.

The use of symbolism will add a richness to the tapestry of the story you are weaving, so it might be well worthwhile to spend a little time considering it.

Tension

Tension, as we've already seen, is inseparable from suspense. It is also closely connected with pace and needs to be considered by itself.

I've just read the manuscript of a novel in which there is some beautiful descriptive writing, setting the scene with deft brushstrokes, an interesting background and believable characters – but very little tension so that two-thirds of the way through I began to skip to get to the end.

To give an example: the main character is attracted to the man who is her boss. We are told this, frequently, but never really *see* how the relationship developed to this point. From time to time he appears, though only briefly. He then comes back on the scene, they make love (although, up until then, she had considered herself committed to another) and, all within the space of a few pages, they are married.

The time element was missing in this story so that everything seemed to be telescoped into an unbelievably short period, though the author probably didn't intend to give that impression. We need to have seen the main character in a number of crisis situations where she had to wrestle with her longing for this man, with her desire to be held in his arms, perhaps when he genuinely wishes to comfort her and to express his growing feeling for her. We should have watched her dawning realisation that what she had thought to be only an infatuation, a physical attraction, was in truth a much deeper love but one she dared not admit because she was promised to someone else. Then the tension would have been stretched, like a piece of elastic, throughout many pages and probably chapters until it was so taut that it threatened to break. Only then should the two lovers have been allowed to come together.

Whenever possible, at the moment you are about to relax that piece of elastic and allow your main character to achieve their goal, prolong the waiting for another few lines, paragraphs or page. If you increase the pressure or, as I once heard it put, 'up the stakes', your story will probably be improved.

Georges Simenon used to say that he drove his characters to extremes and then tested them. By thrusting them into a dilemma, by keeping on turning the screw, forcing them to make choices, decisions, resolving one problem (thus slackening the tension a little) only to have them face even worse difficulties, you will be creating a story that is 'unputdownable'.

Time and transitions

'Once upon a time' is the phrase with which all those well-loved fairy-tales of our childhood begin. Once upon a... time. Because a small child has little conception of time, this is sufficient for his understanding of when the story is set. As adults, however, we require it to be more specific: 'Twelve months ago on this very day...'; 'The eighteenth of June 1987 was the date when...'; 'By Tuesday of the following week, Jamie was...'

Time is like the glue of a story, fixing it firmly into position in the reader's mind. If he isn't told exactly *when* such events occurred, they seem to shift around in a timeless vacuum, leaving him vaguely dissatisfied.

By the same token, the reader needs to know if a period of time has elapsed between one piece of action and the next. This can be indicated by leaving a gap in the text but it is a method which should be used with the discretion, if at all. If used too often throughout a novel, it can prove intensely irritating. The writer should try to find alternative ways of providing this information and specifying the actual length of time that has passed. Mentioning a specific time is also a way of signalling to the reader that it is of special significance and, therefore, should be remembered. For example: 'Dawn was breaking when the wind rose, soughing through the branches of the elms.' This warns that something is about to happen and also paints a picture of the scene for a subsequent piece of action. Often a writer will decide that between the end of one chapter and the start of the next is a good place to allow a lengthy passage of time to occur. This is fine – provided it doesn't result in a loss of tension. The following example illustrates one way this can be accomplished without any slackening.

Wrath, which had been slow to start, began to rise in her. Tonight, however, she would bite her tongue and say noth-

ing, she resolved. But tomorrow... Tomorrow, the fight with
Luke would begin in earnest and she, Catriona, would be the
one to throw down the challenge. (End of chapter)
It was midday before Luke strolled into the house...(Start of
next chapter).

Clearly, several hours have elapsed between Catriona's
resolve to wait till the following day before commencing battle with him, hours during which, presumably, she had gone
to bed, slept, partaken of breakfast and filled in the morning
somehow. But those hours were unimportant to the story's
development and to have dwelt on them would not only have
been unnecessary but would actually have reduced the tension
that was being built up.

Another way of handling it would have been to switch to
the omniscient viewpoint (explained in detail in the section on
Viewpoint), in this way:

But, by midday on June twenty-third, an event of such worldwide proportions had occurred that Catriona's private war
was almost totally eclipsed. Almost, but not quite.

Time, as we've already seen, can also be effectively used to
create tension and suspense by means of the 'time-bomb' technique – when something must be accomplished with a given
period if disaster is to be averted.

By making it clear when a story is taking place (in the present or in the past) and over how long a period, we give it a
framework that helps us visualise the events. The action in Nina
Bawden's *Afternoon of a Good Woman*, for instance, occurs
during the space of a single afternoon (notwithstanding that
much of the story is told through flashback to show us the past
influencing the present).

Transitional passages of any kind are of importance if the
story is to flow smoothly, providing bridges between scenes of
action as well as helping to carry the story forwards. They can
be among the most difficult to write yet, if they are omitted, the
narrative will have a jerky 'feel' to it that will adversely affect
the pace of the story. Nancy Hale in *Realities of Fiction* defines

the transitional passage as being 'a bridge sentence or paragraph...which leads the reader from one time to another, one place to another, or one subject to another in such a way that he is unaware of being budged.'

You can often use a connecting word to link one scene with the next as, for example, 'tomorrow' in the following:

> 'You're so goddammed impetuous, Catriona,' he hurled after her as she spun on her heels and, head held high, stalked from the room. But that he was right, she had to admit, because it was that same impetuosity that was about to pitch her, once again, into the unknown. An unknown in which there would be no Luke to rescue her, to make her feel loved and wanted. Yet, without that impetuous streak in her nature, where would she have been now? She sighed. The point was, she reminded herself soberly, where would she be this time tomorrow? Fifty, or even a hundred, miles south of Barswood perhaps. And alone.

The transitional passage provides a link between the end of one *complete* scene and the next. It gives the reader a little nudge to read on, knowing that more is about to be revealed. I have heard it described as being like the bit of thread you can see between the beads of a necklace.

Perhaps, on those occasions when a story refuses to move forward smoothly (possibly because you need to take a big leap forward in time without dwelling on it in any detail) it might be worth taking a look to see if what is causing the problem is the lack of a transitional passage. If such proves to be the case, writing one in will probably get it moving again for you. In any case, it's worth a try.

Twist in the tale

Stories with a twist in the tail are popular with both readers and writers but they are not as easy to write as many believe. The name of O. Henry, the early twentieth-century American writer who perfected this genre (his first collection of short stories was published in 1904 under the title of *Cabbages and Kings*) has become almost synonymous with it. *The Gift of the Magi*, probably his most famous story, is considered a classic and has a depth that many of this kind do not. Its theme concerns the making of sacrifices for love. In it a young couple each part with their most precious possession (he his gold watch and she her glorious hair) in order to buy a Christmas gift for the other. The twist lies in the final realisation that she has sold her hair in order to buy a chain for his watch while he has sold his watch to buy the tortoise shell combs she coveted.

Another equally famous one with a twist ending is Chekhov's *The Necklace*. A vain woman borrows a valuable necklace to wear at an important function, loses it, has a paste replica made and then spends the next ten years as a drudge in order to replace it, only to learn that the original had been made of paste also.

Roald Dahl's *Tales of the Unexpected*, shown on TV, rely heavily on the twist ending for impact.

Clearly, it is impossible to write this type of story without first knowing what your ending will be because, in effect, you need to work backwards: the end *is* the story. Yet you must never cheat. You cannot have a twist that is conjured up like a rabbit out of a hat. Clues must be carefully and subtly planted throughout. Very often the title itself will provide the first of them and using a well-known phrase or aphorism is a good ploy because it gives a hint as to the solution without being too obvious. One of Roald Dahl's *Tales* is entitled *Lamb to the Slaughter* and revolves around a murder for which the weapon is never found. We learn, at the end, that it was a frozen leg of lamb, which has just been cooked and is about to be eaten, thus destroying the evidence forever.

The object of these stories is to keep the reader guessing until the end and then make him say, chagrined, 'Ah, I should have known!' If you can achieve that reaction, then you will have succeeded.

As a general rule, they are short – 1000/1500 words in length – and are known as 'short shorts'. This is because they depend almost entirely on the element of surprise for effect and not on characterisation or depth of theme.

Most women's magazines like the occasional twist ending, as do other magazines that take fiction. The one notable exception as regards markets is the BBC's *Morning Story*, which does not like them at all.

If you want to try writing them, play around with ideas for plausible surprise endings first, and then work out your plot. If you have the sort of mind that enjoys detective stories where clues are dropped in at judicious intervals while keeping the reader guessing, you might well find you have a talent for writing twist-in-the-tail stories. If this is so, you should have no trouble in selling all you can produce.

Use your knowledge and experience

A writer needs three things, experience, observation and imagination, any two of which, at times any one of which, can supply the lack of the others.

William Faulkner

A maxim you will doubtless have heard many times, if you belong to any kind of writing group, is: write about what you know. It is a wise one, especially applicable in the early stages of your writing life. If you draw upon your own knowledge and experience, your work will have that 'ring of truth', that authenticity that will make it stand out from others when it lands on an editor's desk. This is especially true of non-fiction, of course, but it is just as valid for fiction. With regard to the latter, allowing our characters to live through, and act out, some of our own emotional experiences will not only prove therapeutic for ourselves but will heighten the effect for our readers.

Perhaps this is the reason why so many first novels tend to be autobiographical and why, so often, they prove to be the author's most successful book. Somerset Maugham's *Of Human Bondage* was one such; Hemingway drew upon his experiences in the Spanish Civil War when he was writing *For Whom The Bell Tolls. David Copperfield* owes much to Charles Dickens's boyhood.

Time and again during my creative writing classes I have been amazed and chastened to find that a student whom I had virtually dismissed in my own mind as unlikely to achieve any kind of literary success, produces a piece which, clearly written from the heart and intensely personal, makes a visible impact on the audience. It takes a lot of courage to 'bare one's soul' like this in public and it is a great privilege when I and my class are so trusted. And afterwards that particular student usually finds it easier to write with fewer inhibitions and with greater strength.

Perhaps the biggest hurdle to overcome is realising that what to us is boring, humdrum and everyday knowledge, to someone else is fascinating stuff. To ignore this point is to miss a tailor-made opportunity for success as did, for example, the ex-salesman whose funny (true) stories kept my class in fits of laughter but who insisted on trying to write romances. A similar case was the retired teacher who doggedly refused to write about school-life, preferring fantasy to what he knew in great depth.

It is useful to draw up a list of whatever specialist knowledge you may have, of your work and hobbies and any unusual experiences you've had. 'But,' I hear someone say, 'I only worked in an office for a few years, then I got married, had two children and I've only been a housewife since then.' Now, stop right there and think. You bore two babies, coped with all the problems of pregnancy, infancy, early childhood and adolescence. You certainly know a good deal about being a mother and all that entails so is there some particular knowledge, there, you could pass on to help a young mother of today? Or was there some humorous or unusual incident that would make a reader laugh and sympathise?

A student of mine had arthritis so badly in her hands that she was unable to perform many of the simple tasks that most of us take for granted, including pegging out washing. The only way she could manage this was by putting the clothes-pegs in her mouth and using her teeth. It wasn't until, one day, she saw her small daughter copying her that she realised how odd a practice it really was and yet how perfectly normal it appeared to her little girl. She wrote an article about the funny side of her disability which was snapped up by a glossy magazine within a week.

Having suffered badly from post-natal depression after my daughter was born, years later I sold a piece on this problem (which still exists, unfortunately) to a mother-and-baby magazine.

167

Ask yourself what places you know well. If you've travelled to out-of-the way countries, for instance, you ought to be able to produce an informative and entertaining article that will be readily saleable. Do you know any interesting people whom you could interview, or characters who lived years ago and would make good subjects for character sketches? I remember two such pieces being written by students, one about an old ex-First World War gardener which sold to a Yorkshire paper, the other depicting an elderly football fan which was published in a county magazine. If you hold strong views on a subject, these can often be written up for an opinions or viewpoint slot or slanted to make a controversial piece.

Anything and everything about yourself has potential value as a subject for your writing and you should 'milk' it for all its worth.

Whilst each of us must make our own choice as to the material we shall use, we should, at least, acknowledge the fact that writing about what we know is likely to result in our best work. And isn't that, ultimately, what we all want to achieve?

Vanity publishing

The would-be writer should steer clear of vanity or subsidy publishing, which will involve him or her in laying out a great deal of money (often a four-figure sum) with very little chance of recouping any of it. Aspiring writers, having met with rejection after rejection and desperate to see their work appear in book form, are prime targets for advertisements, often in reputable newspapers, that lure them with blandishments such as: 'publishers seek new authors'. Taking the bait, they submit their completed manuscript (or a synopsis and sample characters), are told it is considered worthy of publication and, finally, asked to part with their money in return for x-number of copies of their book. Unfortunately, despite anything they might be told about possible marketing outlets, the fact remains that bookshops will not handle such material (except, perhaps, for a local author when they might be persuaded to try to sell some on a sale-or-return basis). The author will then find himself left with the vast majority of copies unsold.

If you are considering having your work published in this way, stop and think carefully first. The use of the word 'vanity' says it all: it is just that – vanity at seeing your name in print – but at the cost of expending a large sum of money. Also, from some of the examples I have seen, little or no editing is undertaken by these firms so that glaring grammatical errors, clichés, badly-structured sentences and incorrectly-used words often remain as proof that the author has not yet mastered his craft. Also, bear this in mind: once the glow of seeing all those lovely bound copies of your book has faded and you find that you have most of them still on your hands, an even deeper disappointment will set in. You will have proved absolutely nothing about your writing ability or talent. But, receive a letter of acceptance, followed by a cheque, from a maga-

169

zine editor or a publisher, and you will feel as if you've just conquered Everest. And, if you've done it once, you can do it again.

So, for those of you who are feeling desolated by rejections and are contemplating going to a vanity publisher, my advice is – don't. Apply yourself with even greater determination to learning your craft and be content to break into the bottom end of the magazine and/or newspaper market. Then reap the reward of knowing there are people out there willing to pay good money to read what *you* have written and your self-confidence will receive a well-deserved boost.

Self-publishing is quite different. It may well stem from a certain understandable vanity in wanting to see your work in print, but there the resemblance ends. You have to do everything the publisher would normally do, bearing sole responsibility for the entire procedure, from the writing and editing through to the hiring of a typesetter and the marketing of the finished product. It can be very successful but requires a cool head, organisational abilities of the first order, a prodigious amount of work and the outlay of a large sum of money with the attendant risk of little of it being recouped. I have a copy of a book (the story of a soldier who, in Malaya during the last war, unexpectedly found himself promoted to Major) which was self-published by the author and his wife. In this instance, it paid off and went into a reprint, but it entailed much labour and sales were helped by the fact that it was a tale which interested many ex-soldiers.

Viewpoint

Because viewpoint, more than almost any other aspect of the craft, seems to cause confusion when one starts to write fiction, for ease of understanding we will consider this subject in separate sections. However, before you start to tackle the question of viewpoint at all, you need to decide whose story it is that you intend to tell. That might sound paradoxical but it isn't, in fact. If your plot springs firmly from one particular character, then there is no problem: it will be his/her story. However, if you have a situation in mind from which your plot will evolve, you need to discover which character will meet with the strongest emotional response from your reader.

Let us take the following situation as an example. You think you could write a 'true-life' story around a situation in which a seventeen-year-old girl finds she is pregnant. Clearly, you think, it is the girl's story. But pause for a moment. Does it have to be? That, surely, has been written thousands of times before and hardly lends itself to originality. So, who else might be involved in her predicament? Her mother, almost certainly, so how is she going to feel? Suppose she, too, had had an illegitimate child and had been forced, by circumstances, to part with it straight after its birth. Might not all her past trauma re-surface for her, heightening the poignancy of the present situation? Thus, might not she be the character through whom the strongest feelings could be evoked? And how is the girl's father going to react? His 'little girl' has suddenly grown into a woman and is to become a mother. Perhaps the grandmother also has to face up to the fact that her beloved Jenny is not the pure, innocent child she'd always imagined and she is the one who has to come to terms with a changing approach to sexuality. And, finally, what about the boyfriend, the young man about to be catapulted, through this irresponsibility and immaturity, into becoming a father?

If you consider each of these possibilities in turn, you will probably find that one has more appeal than the others: you will feel more sympathy towards one character than another – and it is that person's story you should tell.

It is interesting to reflect how, from one situation, several plot-lines can be developed. Alan Ayckbourn demonstrated this admirably in his three plays *The Norman Conquests*. It is also worth remembering that, if you are ever desperate for an idea for a short story, you can use this method to find another angle on an already-written story, because it will turn out completely different from the original.

Now we will consider which viewpoint to use in relation to our story.

1. FIRST OR THIRD PERSON SINGULAR

You have your plot idea, you know your main character and now you have to decide on whether to use the first or the third person viewpoint. It would be a rare novel (and never a short story) that could sustain a change in mid-stream though doubtless it has been done in the past and will be in the future by accomplished practitioners. For our purposes, however, we want to increase our chances of success by concentrating on techniques that are as simple to handle as possible, concomitant with producing a readable book of as high a standard as we can accomplish.

The 'I' has definite advantages in the telling of certain types of story. The so-called 'confession' or 'true-life' story already referred to must, by definition, be related in this way. I, the narrator, am confiding in you, the reader: I am confessing my misdemeanours, my sins, my mistakes in the hope that you will learn from what happened to me and won't commit the same errors. In this way, a strong bond is created between narrator and reader which makes you hang on every word.

Imagine you are walking down the street, one day, when a friend comes up to you, grabs you by the arm and whispers hoarsely, 'Oh, Joanne, guess what I did last night? I know I shouldn't have and if Gary ever finds out...' You'd be an unusual person if your ears weren't instantly flapping to hear the rest. But, if the same friend started to tell you about someone called Samantha and what she did, unless you knew her personally, you'd only be listening with half an ear. It's the 'I' that captures your attention.

Writers of gothic and romantic-suspense novels tend to use this viewpoint, too. Think of *Jane Eyre*, that prototype of the gothic genre; of *Rebecca* by Daphne du Maurier, and those books by Mary Stewart and Phyllis Whitney. The 'I' has an immediacy that hooks you from the first sentence: you are *there*, drawn into the events that are plunging the heroine into danger and emotional turmoil.

Now to the main disadvantage. This is simply that we, the readers, can only know what the narrator would know through her own five senses. We cannot learn about any happening from another character, nor enter into their thoughts. Nor can you ever stand back and make authorial comment. In this respect, the first person viewpoint is restrictive and it is up to you to decide whether or not its advantages will most help the particular story you are engaged upon.

There are many ways, of course, by which you can convey another's thoughts. 'I shot him a direct glance and thought I caught a furtive gleam in those dark eyes before they were shuttered by heavy lids.' We are now quite certain there is something suspicious about the other character but only because the 'I' has sensed it. 'She watched me with what could have been nervousness' (*The Moonspinners* by Mary Stewart).

You can also suggest what might be happening out of sight of the narrator: 'In my mind's eye I could see him standing, as before, with the glasses to his eyes, raking the crannies and cliffs above him for a possible hiding-place.' (*The Moonspinners*)

When you commence your short story or novel, you may well begin in the third person from the angle of your main character but something doesn't seem quite right: it isn't flowing as you would wish. At that point, it is worth considering the possibility that it might work better in the first. Sometimes that is all that is needed to get it steaming ahead.

2. OTHER AVAILABLE VIEWPOINTS

We have already discussed the third person as main character and the first person as narrating main character, but there is also the 'I' as minor character to be looked at, even though it is used infrequently. H. E. Bates uses this form in his famous *Uncle Silas* stories. Uncle Silas undoubtedly is the main character but they are related by his nephew, the 'I'.

There is yet a fourth viewpoint, the omniscient, sometimes known as the god's eye view. This latter is unlikely to succeed in the short story as it is too detached (literally, the god is gazing down and commenting on what is taking place below). It is often employed, however, during the course of a novel.

To illustrate the four viewpoints, let us take a situation where a man, John Spence, returns home from the office, one evening, to find his wife gone and his home virtually stripped bare and see it from each one.

John Spence as main character – third person

When John Spence arrived home from work, that Monday night, he couldn't believe his eyes. The house was as empty as if someone had been through it with a gigantic vacuum cleaner and sucked everything out. What on earth had happened? And where, he asked himself, was Ethel?

John Spence as main character narrator – first person

When I got home from work, that Monday night, I couldn't believe my eyes. The house was as empty as if someone has been through it with a gigantic vacuum cleaner. What on earth had happened? And where, I asked myself, was Ethel?

Narrator as minor character

I was with John Spence when he got home from work, that Monday night. His house was completely empty like someone had been through it with... And when he turned to me as if seeking some kind of explanation, I knew this was one situation I couldn't wriggle out of. Somehow, I had to try and help.

The 'I' as minor character must be involved in the story, otherwise you fall into the trap of relating a 'story within a frame' which is extremely old-fashioned and unlikely to sell. This type often used to start off a ghost story where a group of men are sitting round a fire in an old inn and one of them starts to relate an eerie story.

The omniscient viewpoint

No one ever knew the real reason why John Spence's wife left home – they only knew he got back from work, one Monday night, to find the house stripped bare and Ethel gone. The neighbours, naturally enough, were puzzled by it all – and even more so when they heard him singing around the place, the following morning, his cheerful bass voice echoing in the emptiness.

3. VIEWPOINT IN RELATION TO (A) THE NOVEL AND (B) THE SHORT STORY

We need to look at viewpoint, in this context, separately because of the vast difference in the two genres.

(a) The novel

As has already been said, in respect of the novel, if you decide on the first person, then you should stick to it throughout its length. If you choose the third person (and by far the greatest number employ this) you can write from the angle of each and any of the characters in your book: that is, use multiple third person viewpoint, which is the most common method in full-length fiction. You do need to be aware, however, of the danger of switching too often within one chapter for the reason mentioned earlier: your aim is to build up sympathy towards each character. It is all too easy to allow this to be dissipated by moving from one viewpoint to another *without having a good reason for so doing*. Therein lies the secret: know what you are doing – and why. In other words, having learned your craft, use it to its full advantage.

You may well, too, use the omniscient view, from time to time, to fill in necessary detail and comment on what is taking place in the novel, though not in conjunction with the first person or this would lead to that suspension of disbelief remarked upon by Samuel Coleridge Taylor.

If you critically analyse any published novel, you can observe all this in operation for yourself: indeed, it is imperative, during the learning process, to do just this.

(b) The short story

It is here that the real difficulty seems to lie with beginner-writers until they have grasped the concept of this genre's tight structure (see pp. 135-45). It is sufficient to state here that, as a general rule, the short story should be told from one view-point throughout its entirety. This will maximise the emotional response that you are aiming to effect in your reader. In a piece of fiction of between, say, 1000 and 5000 words, changing is likely to reduce this response by diffusing it. A golden rule is never to slip from one character's viewpoint to another's unless your story gains more from it than it loses.

Finally, if you can once get right into the skin of your main character and *stay there* for the duration of your story, you should not find yourself unintentionally slipping out of your chosen viewpoint.

Why?

'Why' is the most important word in a fiction writer's vocabulary. Without an insatiable curiosity about what makes people tick, and a wish to understand why someone has acted in a certain way, it's unlikely we'll be able to write a good story. It is the 'why', i.e. motivation, that provides the mainspring of all fiction.

Motivation (from the Latin verb *movere*, to move) causes all action; without it, nothing at all would happen. In life we don't always know the reason someone does something. That nice quiet man down the street kills his wife and the neighbours are stunned: they cannot understand why. Hadn't he always seemed a pleasant, mild-mannered man? They may never know the truth but, if this occurred in fiction, we have to know. We will feel cheated if the motivation isn't made clear and the build-up to the murder shown. Therefore, as writers, we must know exactly why a character behaves in such an *apparently* uncharacteristic fashion if the story is to work.

Suppose, for instance, that this man, Henry Smith, has been a model railway enthusiast all his life. Then he gets married and, after a while, his wife begins to nag about the time he spends in the loft with his beloved trains. One day they have a terrible row and she threatens to leave him unless he gets rid of them. He ignores her, goes off to work and, on his return, finds she hasn't left but, instead, has smashed up his train set. Provided we have seen his growing obsession with it, we can begin to believe in the terrible revenge he wreaks. But, to make his action entirely credible, we need to delve even deeper. Why hasn't he outgrown and put away his childhood toy? Is it, perhaps, because of a refusal to grow up, to change, to accept the responsibilities of adulthood? Did he, in fact, marry in the expectation that his wife would go on letting him be a little boy?

Was the real reason for the murder that she tried to force him to change and he would not?

It is by the constant asking of 'why?' that we throw more light upon the characters we have created, discover what motivates them and so make them rounder and less of cardboard cut-outs. And, as a consequence, we will make our readers more willing to suspend their disbelief in our piece of fiction.

Word count

There is a simple but effective method of calculating the length of a typescript. Publishers and editors use this to find out how much actual space a piece will take up.

1   Count the number of words in 25 *full-length* lines, then find the average number of words per line by dividing the total by 25. For example, 292 words divided by 25 equals 11.6 words per line.

2   Count the number of lines on a page (they should remain the same for each one) and multiply by the average number of words per line: 30 lines multiplied by 11.6 equals 348 words per page.

3   Count the number of pages in the typescript and multiply by the number of words per page: 221 pages multiplied by 348 words equals 76,908 or approximately 77,000 words.

(Note that for the purposes of printing, part pages and part lines occupy the same amount of space as full pages and full lines.)

Working methods

Every day some words.

Emile Zola

Methods will obviously vary between individuals. However, there are certain factors common to practically every successful writer (and definitely to every professional one). These must be worth considering.

You must write regularly, however little time you can set aside each day. Make a pact with yourself to write a minimum of words daily, if possible, or weekly, if not. To start with, don't set yourself too big a task or you maybe overstretched and give up. 100 words a day, as highly-polished as you can make them, add up to 700 a week or two pages of a book; not too big a target for most.

Write at the same time each day, if possible. The mind, like children and animals, responds to routine and its working mechanism seems to spring into action far more readily if its inner alarm-clock is set for, say, seven each morning or seven each night. This brings up, naturally, the bogey of most writers – self-discipline.

The need for structure in our lives is of great psychological moment and, when we go to work, to office, shop, factory or wherever, we have such a structure imposed upon us and accept it, albeit with resignation, Then, thinking we'd like to become writers and dreaming of the sheer bliss of being our own master, of having the whole day in which to write, we convince ourselves it is but time we need in order to become successful. It's easy for those who write full-time, we tell ourselves. We'd soon have our name on a book-jacket if we could only sit at as desk from 9 to 5 and do nothing but write.

180

Oh, what a rude awakening lies ahead for those who think like that. I know – I've been there – and so have many others. The sun is shining after days of rain so I'd better do the laundry and get it out to dry, I think...and I ought to give the dog a run whilst it's nice... A friend phones: she's had a tiff with her husband and needs someone to confide in – me – so I can't possibly refuse, can I? The list of excuses is endless – but that's what they are, excuses.

There is no answer to this except your own determination but I will pass on to you my own theory (an insight gained by ruthless self-examination) as to why so many of us put off getting down to our writing. I believe it is purely and simply a fear of failure. If we never actually put our work to the test, never finish that novel or play and submit it to a publisher, we can go on deluding ourselves that we could be as good as the next – if only we had the time!

. We need to face this and deal with it sternly. Deadlines undoubtedly help. I had a deadline to meet for this book, and it created a subtle, and then not so subtle pressure, as completion date approached. Setting your own deadline, if you haven't a commission to complete, is a good way of keeping you at the desk.

You may find some small habit or gimmick will help. Start the day by sharpening your pencils like Hemingway. Write a letter to a friend as did John Steinbeck. Read through what you wrote the day before; you'll soon be in the right frame of mind to begin.

What method to use for the actual writing: longhand, typewriter or that piece of high-technology that is sweeping through the writing world – the word processor? Really, it's a matter of personal choice. Many find that a machine is too impersonal and blocks their creativity while, for others, the typewriter is quicker and wastes less time. But the word processor has become the talking point at any gathering of writers and, almost without exception, they swear they wouldn't be without theirs. But – there is always a but – bear in mind that it is only a piece of equipment: it won't create a successful short story or novel for you: it won't put the right words in the right order for

181

you. If your spelling is weak, it can correct it by using special dictionary software, but don't depend on it. If you've used the wrong word, but spelt it correctly, the machine won't know! It will save endless time in your re-writing once you've mastered its complexities. Indeed, I heard one novelist proclaim that this had saved him more than two months' work in the revision of a long novel, time which, for a professional writer, means money.

Another but: depending upon your aptitude, word-processors can take a while to understand, so it probably isn't advisable to try to use one if you are in the middle of a long piece of work. Wait until your undoubted frustration won't be reflected in your writing.

Finally, only you can find, by trial and error, which is the best method for you. But at least be honest with yourself: no excuses about lack of time or unsuitable place. Wherever, however and whenever, if you have the determination and perseverance, you will succeed whatever working methods you choose.

Writing groups and courses

I think there is little doubt that belonging to a writing group of some kind, be it a circle or a class such as one run by your local education authority or the Workers' Education Association, is a great help, especially when you are beginning. Being in the company of other writers and would-be writers provides a stimulus that is usually missing if you are working in isolation. You will also have the advantage of having a piece of writing criticised (this should always be constructive, of course) and the valuable feedback from members of the group as well as receiving some actual instruction in technique.

With regard to correspondence courses such as are advertised in the press, these are usually only as good as the individual tutor assigned to you. Their main advantage is that they make you write, but their disadvantage is that you have no direct personal contact with your tutor. A high percentage of students never actually finish the course (and, therefore, are not eligible for a refund of fees, where that is offered), many, doubtless, discovering that writing is not as easy as they had first thought.

For those who are unable or unwilling to consider other options, I hope this *A to Z* will provide the solution.

A list of writers' circles all over the country has been compiled by Jill Dick and the address of where to obtain it will be found at the back of this book.

'Xtra

Yes – I've had to cheat a little, here, to find a subject beginning with X. However, unless you can give your story that something extra to lift it above the rest, it's not likely to succeed in today's highly competitive marketplace. It is a carefully thought out 'plus-factor' that will make your novel or short story stand out from all the others that land on an editor's desk.

In the eighteenth century Georges Polti worked out that there are only a limited number of basic plots available to a writer. His list, *The Thirty-six Dramatic Situations*, has become famous and is frequently reproduced in print. If his theory is correct, it goes to prove the paramount importance of originality in choice of character, setting and situation in every piece of fiction.

We've already seen the need for creating characters who are flesh and blood and not cardboard cut-outs, so we know we must have a main character who will arouse our reader's interest and sympathy. But we must also find an unusual setting or background that hasn't been used a thousand times before and bring that to life, too. And you will only be able to do that if you use one with which you are familiar or which you have researched in depth. This is what will give your story that element previously mentioned – immediacy – and also that vital 'plus factor'.

Take a critical look at some of the books that have been bestsellers or stories that have become classics and try to identify what made them so outstanding. Scarlett O'Hara and Rhett Butler were both larger-than-life figures but, without that vivid depiction of the American Civil War and its aftermath, would Margaret Mitchell's book have been so successful? If Jane Austen had not been so familiar with the social strata and background of early nineteenth-century upper-class England, its mores and customs, would her books have survived? There have been stories about characters who live in a fantasy world both before and after James Thurber wrote *The Secret Life of Walter Mitty*, but something about that particular character and his dreams made Thurber's story unforgettable.

When you are in the planning stage of your short story or novel, but especially the latter, think long and hard about what could give it that extra dimension that will make an editor sit up and read it with especial attention. If, for example, it is basically a love story – boy meets girl; boy loses girl; boy finds girl again – there would appear to be nothing particularly new about that plot. However, set it in India at the time of the British Raj, have a number of exciting and terrifying ordeals befall your hero and heroine before they are finally brought together to live 'happily ever after' and you will have given your story a fascinating and colourful background that will hold your reader's interest until the last page. You may even find you have written another *Far Pavilions* that will make the bestseller lists and make you and your publisher millions!

So, to inject your story with that something extra, consider the following points:

1   Use settings with which you are familiar or which you are able to research in depth so that they spring to life and make the reader feel he is there with you.

2   Give your characters careers or backgrounds which are interesting and unusual and with which you are familiar or, again, which you can research in depth. For example, Dick Francis uses a 'horsey' background over and over again because he knows it intimately and he has found that his readers love it. Some of the most successful writers of romantic novels consistently use those with which few of their readers will be familiar and, therefore, will find of interest (racing stables, deepsea diving, journalism, the world of artists, sculptors, fashion-models, photographers and so on). It is this which, apart from their evident writing skills, has lifted their books out of the limbo of being 'as good as' those hundreds of others submitted in hope to a publisher.

3   Lastly, however slight your story, let it have something to say; have some meaning for the reader.

Add one or more of these factors to your story and you will have given it that 'xtra something that will help lift it out of the 'slush-pile' and into print.

Young adult or teenage fiction

Fiction for young adults comes into a category of its own but, for fairly obvious reasons, it is a narrow one. Children who have an advanced reading age will probably progress almost directly from children's to adult fiction while teenage boys tend to be more interested in 'doing' than in reading. Nevertheless, the category does exist for those interested in writing for it.

A sub-genre that is proving very popular with girls of this age is the paperback romance and every library carries a selection. 'Heartlines' published by Pan Books are among the best written and consist of British-based stories. 'Sweet Dreams' by Bantam are American-based with no opening for UK authors, at present. Grafton Books (a Collins imprint) produce an historical romance series under the title 'Dawn of Love', some of which are excellently written. Another current imprint for this age group is Puffin Plus.

There are other publishers and series catering for young adults but often enough they appear, flourish for a time and then fade away so it is necessary to keep alert to what is happening in the market by talking to librarians, browsing through bookshops and obtaining lists from publishers.

There is also a vast market for short stories in magazines aimed at teenage girls.

If you want to write for young adults, you need to be in touch with them in order to be able to observe their attitudes, behaviour, language, modes of dress and appearance. But their problems, secret longings, heartaches will differ little from those we have all experienced at the same period in our lives because they are changeless. What is considerably different is the pressure that a much faster pace of life has brought, the enormous problem of unemployment for so many, the dangers of trying to escape by means of drug-taking and drink. If you can't identify with these young people of today, empathise with their very real difficulties, then forget about trying to write for and about them.

Young adult fiction is about a voyage of self-discovery, about learning of ways to cope and grow up in an often all-too-confusing world where those in authority over them never seem to have time to listen or to try to understand. They will be experiencing loneliness, feelings of isolation, grief, rejection (quite possibly through parents divorcing or having been turned down for job after job) amongst other confusing emotions.

We live in a multi-racial, multi-cultural society today, with its own special areas of conflict which have to be faced by many young people growing up. This cannot, and should not, be ignored in fiction. However, if you are white, unless you are very close to someone of another race or culture, it would smack of arrogance to try to write from their viewpoint. You could do it from a white child's standpoint, though, perhaps facing the prejudice that might well exist because of friendship with someone of a different shade of skin. I once wrote a story for a teenage magazine on this subject. My main character was a young man who has a black girlfriend. He was under pressure from peers and family to give her up. He bowed to that pressure and split with her, only to realise how much he missed her and how foolish he had been to listen to others. He tried to make it up but it was too late: her trust in him had gone.

Think yourself back to those adolescent years and try to recall what your feelings were. Did you feel stupid, ugly or inarticulate, that you didn't belong, weren't loved or accepted? Then transpose those emotions to the standpoint of a young person of today and write from that and not from the adult you are now.

Short teenage fiction is a good training ground for longer works and D. C. Thomson's three magazines, *Jackie, Patches* and *Blue Jeans*, have been around for many years, reflecting life for that age group. Many of their short stories (known as 'Reader's True Experiences' or RTEs) are really mini-confessions in which the main character (usually a girl but occasionally a boy) behaves badly in some way, suffers because of it and finally realises her mistake. Sometimes she realises it in time and escapes retribution; at others, she isn't so lucky and suffers the consequences, finally resolving never to act like that again. Studying the problem pages will help you find likely topics on which to base your stories.

Another magazine catering for an older, more worldly-wise kind of girl is *Just Seventeen*. This is much more sophisticated but it pays very well and, judging by the speed with which it disappears from the magazine racks, is exceedingly popular.

Whether you are writing a short story or a novel for the young adult, the secret of success lies in reader identification. The reader will empathise and see how the main character copes with a similar problem to that which she is also experiencing. By the end she will have learned a little more about life. Whilst a conventional 'happy ending' is not necessary (apart from the romances), the end should definitely be on a note of hope, of optimism.

A type of fiction which is becoming increasingly popular with boys of this age-group is the 'Dungeons and Dragons' variety and 'game books'. If you want to write for them, it would be worth studying some of these.

Because imprints come and go, it is essential to keep an eye on market trends and what is currently available.

Yourself

In the end, it is *your* story, your book, your piece of writing.
You've read and listened to advice and criticism and now you
must stand back, survey it honestly and as objectively as possible and make your own decision: either change it in the light of
this or leave it as it is. It is up to you.

Zeal and Zest

If you pursue your writing hobby with zeal, who knows, it may well turn into a career. One writer I know persevered for several years without selling a single piece but she didn't let it bother her: she realised she was learning her craft. Then she began to have a few articles and short stories accepted, progressed to romantic novels and now, late on in life, has more than a dozen novels to her credit, most from an illustrious publishing house – and her zest never dimishes. May it be the same with you.

Bibliography

Thesaurus of English Words and Phrases, P. M. Roget, ed. F. M. Kirkpatrick. Longman, 1987.

Shorter Oxford English Dictionary. Oxford University Press, 1973.

Writers' and Artists' Year Book. A. & C. Black.

The Writer's Handbook, ed. B. Turner. Macmillan.

The Oxford Dictionary of Quotations. Oxford University Press, 1979.

The Penguin Dictionary of Quotations. Penguin.

Brewer's Dictionary of Phrase and Fable, ed. I Evans. Cassell.

The Way to Write Radio Drama, William Ash. Hamish Hamilton, 1985.

The Art of Dramatic Writing, Lajos Egri. Simon & Schuster, 1946.

Writers at Work: The 'Paris Review' Interviews, ed. G. Plimpton. Secker & Warburg/Penguin.

A Handbook of Copyright in British Publishing Practice, J. M. Cavendish. Cassell, 1984.

Publishing Agreements: A Book of Precedents, Charles Clark. Allen & Unwin, 1984.

The Writer's Handbook, ed. A. S. Burack. The Writer Inc., USA.

Research for Writers, Ann Hoffmann. A. & C. Black, 1986.

The Realities of Fiction, Nancy Hale. Macmillan, 1963.

Guide to Fiction Writing, Phyllis Whitney. Poplar Press, 1984.

A Writer's Notebook, Somerset Maugham. Heinemann, 1951.

The Making of a Novelist, Margaret Thomson Davis. Allison & Busby, 1981.

The Art of Writing, André Maurois. The Bodley Head, 1960.

Reader's Report, Christopher Derrick. Gollancz, 1969.

Writing Historical Fiction, Rhona Martin. A. & C. Black, 1988.

The Modern Short Story, H. E. Bates. Michael Joseph.

The Short Story, Sean O'Faoláin. Mercier Press, 1973.

How to Write the Story of Your Life, Frank P. Thomas. Writer's Digest Books, 1986.

Story Writing, Edith Ronald Mirrielees. The Writer Inc., USA, 1947.

The Art of Writing Made Simple, Geoffrey Ashe. Heinemann, 1972.

The Craft of Writing Articles, Gordon Wells. Allison & Busby, 1983.

How to Write for Children, Tessa Krailing. Allison & Busby, 1988.

The 'Rebecca' Notebook and Other Memories, Daphne du Maurier. Gollancz, 1981.

Creative Writing, Julia Casterton. Macmillan, 1986.

Danse Macabre, Stephen King. Futura, 1982.

The Anatomy of Poetry, Marjorie Boulton. Routledge & Kegan Paul, 1953.

The number of books on the subject of writing, either in general or in particular, is almost endless and provides delight and fascination for anyone interested in writing or literature. Many books are now out of print but one can often come across them in secondhand bookshops – it's like finding treasure-trove. Good reading.

Useful addresses

The Society of Authors
84 Drayton Gardens
London SW10 9SB

Writers' Guild of Great Britain
430 Edgware Road,
London W2 1EH

Society of Women Writers & Journalists
Hon. Sec. Olive Macdonald
2 St Lawrence Close
Edgware
Middlesex HA8 6RB (Probationary members accepted.)

The Romantic Novelists' Association
Hon. Treasurer, Marina Oliver
Half Hidden,
West Lane,
Nr Princes Risborough,
Bucks HP17 9PF (Probationary members accepted.)

P.E.N.
7 Dilke Street
London SW3 4JE

The Poetry Society
21 Earls Court Square
London SW5 9DE

British Science Fiction Association
33 Thornville Road
Hartlepool
Cleveland TS26 8EW

Book Trust,
Book House
45 East Hill
London SW18 2QZ

The Arvon Foundation
Totleigh Barton
Sheepwash
Devon EX21 5NS
(Short writing courses run at this address and also in Yorkshire.)

Writers' Holiday,
Administrator, Anne Hobbs
30 Pant Road
Newport
Gwent
(Held annually in South Wales in July.)

Writers' Summer School
Hon. Sec., Philippa Boland
The Red House
Mardens Hill
Crowborough
Sussex TN6 1XN
(Held annually in August.)

Useful publications

Freelance Market News, 5/9 Bexley Square, Salford, Manchester M3 6DN

Writers' Monthly, 18/20 High Road, London N22 6DN

The Writer and *Writer's Digest* (both American publications), available from Freelance Press Services, 5/9 Bexley Square, Manchester M3 6DB

Writing for the BBC (BBC Books)

Success magazine, 17 Andrew's Crescent, Peterborough PE4 6XE

Quartos magazine, BCM–Writer, London WC1N 3XX

Writing Today, 109 Redlam, Blackburn BB1 1UN

Writing, 87 Brookhouse Road, Farnborough, Hants GU14 0BU

Directory of Writers' Circles, compiled by Jill Dick, available from Oldacre, Horderns Park Road, Chapel-en-le-Frith, Derbyshire SK12 6SY

Freelance Writing & Photography, Victoria House, Victoria Road, Hale, Cheshire WA15 0RB

Writers News, David & Charles, Brunel House, Newton Abbot, Devon TQ12 4YG

Competitions

Literary competitions continue to proliferate, both locally and nationally. Their main advantage, it seems to me, is that they provide that often necessary spur to, as Sinclair Lewis once put it, 'apply the seat of your pants to the seat of your chair' and write. A deadline is something writers often need so entering literary competitions provides a self-imposed discipline which can only be helpful.

If you belong to a circle or class, you will be probably hear of most, if not all, of them. If you are writing in isolation, you will have to ask friends and family to keep eyes and ears open for news of any and you will need to watch for announcements in the press, and regularly scour the magazines on newsagents' shelves, to spot any being advertised. To give you some idea of the number and scope of those that have been run, in recent years (some of which are annual events), the following is a list of just a few of them, large and small.

BBC Radio – Drama
Mobil Oil – Drama
The Mail on Sunday – opening of a novel
Bridport – Short story and poetry
Swanage Arts Festival – Short story and poetry
Dillington – Short story (regional: South-west)
Woman's Own – Short story
The Sunday Times – Travel writing
Woman's Journal – Short story
Saga magazine – Short story
Saga magazine – Travel article
Stand magazine – Short story
She – Opening of a romantic novel (in conjunction with Corgi)
The Sunday Express/Veuve Clicquot – Short story
Chelston Citroen (South West Book Fair) – Short story

Many writers' circles organise competitions, either local or nationwide, to raise funds for their circle. Among these are:
Crediton Writers' Circle – Short story/poetry
Isle of Wight Writers' Circle – Short story

197

South & Mid-Wales Association of Writers – Radio play

Various publications which try to keep entrants informed about current competitions include:

Quartos magazine, BCM–Writer, London WC1N 3XX
Writers' Monthly, 18/20 High Road, London N22 6DN
Freelance Market News, 5/9 Bexley Square, Manchester
Writers News, David & Charles, Brunel House, Newton Abbot, Devon TQ12 4YG

Finally, some points to remember when entering competitions because, if you ignore them, you risk being disqualified:

1   Invariably, there will be a stipulated length (words, time for a play, lines for poetry). You must make sure your entry does not exceed that.

2   If a pseudonym is asked for make sure your own name does not appear on your entry.

3   Keep a copy for yourself in case the original is not returned.

Index